Raising Charlie

The Lessons of a Perfect Dog

John Lichty

Copyright © 2009 by John Lichty
All rights reserved.

No part of this book may be reproduced, stored in a retrieval system or transmitted by any means without the written permission of the author.

ISBN: 978-0-982-68081-0

To Charlie, my perfect dog

And to Nan, who encouraged me
to write his story

Contents

Introduction xi

Raising Charlie 1

New Year's Eve 15

Tests and More Tests 23

Fort Collins Diagnosis 31

Living with Cancer 41

The Last Good Days 51

Denver Debacle 79

Birthday 91

The End 99

The Lessons of a Perfect Dog 111

Reflections 123

Epilogue: Raising Scout 133

A dog wags its tail with its heart.

— Martin Buxbaum

Introduction

THIS IS THE STORY OF CHARLIE, a special dog, perhaps even a perfect dog—and not just because he was my dog. If you asked the people who knew him, they would probably agree. You can read their comments later, in the Reflections chapter near the end of this book.

Between here and there, you will learn about what made Charlie who he was and why it is important for me to write about his life. Because, you see, Charlie died in April 2008, right after his tenth birthday, and much too soon for a companion we thought would be a part of our lives for another three to five years. Not a day goes by that I don't think about Charlie and how much I miss him, sometimes with watering eyes and a lump in my throat. That is why his story has been so difficult for me to write. It is emotionally upsetting to replay the final three months of Charlie's life in my mind and try to make sense of them in writing. I prefer to think and write about the good days, the days before his diagnosis, and the wonderful adventures we shared together. But to appreciate the fullness of Charlie's character, the whole story needs to be told.

My hope for you, the reader, is that you take away something valuable from the example of Charlie's life. Even if you are not a dog owner, there is much to be learned about love, trust and the special bond that forms between people and their dogs.

A dog is not just a reflection of his owner; it works both ways. To understand a dog, you must meet in the middle, where you are also a reflection of him. That is when true character is revealed, when you see the world and your place in it from the perspective of a life more wild and natural than your own.

But that is just one of many lessons learned from Charlie. The lessons are why I owe it to him to tell his story, because I know that I am a better person for having had him in my life.

Dogs are not our whole life, but they make our lives whole.

— Roger Caras

Raising Charlie

CHARLIE WAS BORN TO A SMALL private breeder who lived south of Silt, Colorado. Annie owned one male golden retriever and two females. Both females gave birth at about the same time, one to a litter of ten and the other to a litter of eleven. Twenty-one puppies in all! Charlie was the ninth puppy in the litter of ten born to Jenny Dancing Bear on March 29, 1998. Charlie's father was Annie's male, Tuff Red Rock, named for his strong-willed nature.

A couple of weeks before my fortieth birthday, right around the end of May, my wife, Nan, put a copy of the *Aspen Daily News* classified ads in front of me as I was eating my Sunday breakfast. She pointed to an ad under the heading of Animals for Sale: "Golden retriever puppies. Ready now." I looked up at her with inquiring eyes.

She said, "I wanted to get you something special for your fortieth. What do you think? Do you want to maybe just go and look at them?"

I thought about it for a moment and then replied, "Sure. Let's go take a look."

We called the number in the ad and talked with Annie. She told us there were only four puppies left, so if we wanted to see them, we should drive down right away.

When we arrived at Annie's house, she and her husband, Pat, welcomed us into their kitchen, which they had partitioned off with boards to prevent the puppies from wandering. Another woman was also there to look at the puppies and was holding one in her arms. Nan and I knelt down to look at the other three. Two were sleeping soundly, but one was stirring. He was the cutest of the bunch, so I gently picked him up and placed him on his feet. He stretched and shivered a little and then looked up at us with bright brown eyes. We were enchanted. He moved closer to us and then tried to climb over the partition. I lifted him over and placed him on the floor. He began nosing around in every direction. We asked Annie if we could take him outside. "Yes," she said, "but be careful. That one's strong-willed, just like his father." We agreed to keep a close eye on him.

I picked him up and tucked him under my arm like a football as we walked out the back door. I set him down, and he immediately started making a beeline for the front of the house, but at a puppy's pace. Nan and I trailed after him, asking the inevitable questions:

Me: What do you think of him?

Nan: He's really cute, but I don't know. What do you think?

Me: I'm not sure. Are we ready to have a puppy?

And we came up with the expected rationalizations:

Me: I know we were coming here only to look, but if we leave without him, somebody else will get him.

Nan: It's up to you. He's your birthday present.

That decided it. Before the puppy reached the road in front of the house, I picked him up, and we walked back to the house to talk with

Annie. She gave us the rundown: "He's nine weeks old. He's AKC. He's had all his vaccinations. And he's yours for $300." Nan must have been thinking ahead to this possibility because she had that amount in cash. Annie gave us the puppy's health record, showing the dates of his vaccinations, and the forms we would need to register him with the American Kennel Club. She wished us luck, and we drove away, the proud new owners of a golden retriever puppy.

My birthday puppy was our second golden retriever. Our first was Rollie, born in August 1991. We named him after my grandfather Roland Lichty, my father's father, and also after the chubby puppy in the Disney film, *One Hundred and One Dalmatians*. Like Charlie, Rollie was a gift, a wedding present from my brother and sisters. They knew that I had always wanted a dog, so they gave us money along with a card telling us to spend it on one. Nan and I were married on June 2, 1989, and it took us a little over two years to locate a puppy. We were living in Aspen, Colorado—an extremely dog-friendly town—and were exposed to lots of different dogs. Several people we knew owned golden retrievers, the unofficial mascot of Aspen, and they seemed like really nice dogs. I still remember a few by name: PJ, Penny, Winston and Buzz. So it was familiarity with the breed more than anything that had us hoping we might be able to find a golden puppy.

Nan's sister Sue lived about an hour and a half away in Edwards with her husband, Jack. Sue was organizing a rummage sale one weekend in the fall of 1991, and we went over to help her and to sell some of our own stuff. Maria from up the road came by and mentioned that her golden retriever, Ginger, had given birth to a litter of puppies a few weeks before. She said we should stop by to look at them. The puppies were only four weeks old, but Nan and I knew we had finally found our wedding-present puppy. We returned three weeks later to pick him up.

Rollie was a wonderful little puppy, but our relationship with him was doomed. Our condominium association had a bylaw prohibiting dogs, but the woman three doors down moved in with a schnauzer, so we figured that the bylaw was just being ignored. We were wrong. The association came down so hard on us that we were faced with major penalties if we didn't give Rollie up. It was an obvious case of selective enforcement, but we weren't in the financial position to fight it. Fortunately for us, Sue and Jack stepped in to adopt Rollie, and he ended up living only a quarter-mile down the road from where he was born.

Nan and I learned an important lesson from this experience: always check with whatever agency governs your living situation to be absolutely sure that dogs are permitted on the premises before you consider bringing one into your home. Failure to do so may result in penalties, eviction and heartbreak.

Rollie was ours for only about four months, but they were valuable months for him and for us. We had picked up a golden retriever pet owner's manual at a pet shop and read it carefully in the time between meeting Rollie and picking him up. We thought that we were ready for the challenges of housebreaking and training, but Rollie kept us on our toes the entire time. What we learned from him, our starter dog, we were able to apply much more effectively to Charlie almost six years later.

Nan and I knew that we were unprepared when we drove away from Annie's house that spring day in 1998, but that didn't lessen the excitement for us. Our new puppy was even more excited. He sat in a cardboard box on Nan's lap whining and howling at the sudden separation from his mother, his littermates and the life he had known. While Nan tried to calm him, I brought up the idea of naming him Charlie. It was a name I had liked for a dog since reading John Steinbeck's *Travels with Charley*, and like Rollie, it was a family name. Two of my great grandfathers, one on each side of the family, had been named Charles: Charles Yardley on my father's side and Charles Ethan Allen on my mother's. Nan reminded me that the puppy was my birthday present, so it was up to me to name him. Charlie it was.

We drove straight to a Wal-Mart to buy the things we would need. Nan went inside with a shopping list, while I sat on the tailgate of our SUV with Charlie at my side, a comforting arm around his little body. He was calm by then and watching with bright, curious eyes the steady stream of people, shopping carts and cars. When he became fidgety, I sensed that he needed to pee, so I carried him over to a patch of grass at the edge of the parking lot. He promptly squatted and peed, which prompted me to say, "Good boy!" We were off to a good start.

When we arrived home, I carried Charlie to the back corner of our yard and set him down. He sniffed around the grass and then went into a hopping, spinning squat to poop. "Good boy!" This housebreaking is going to be a cinch, I thought, as I carried him up the stairs and into the house.

Nan was unpacking our new puppy stuff in the kitchen. "He's probably hungry," she said. "I'll get some food ready for him." I set Charlie down to let him explore while I filled his water dish at the sink. Nan went to work making a warm mash of some puppy chow, which is what Annie had been feeding the puppies. When we set the dishes down in a designated corner of the kitchen, Charlie ran right over and started eating as fast as he could. He had been competing with his littermates at a communal bowl, so he was accustomed to eating quickly to get as much food as possible. It took several days for him to realize that he was going to get all the food in his dish and that he could eat more slowly.

As I sat in the living room assembling the new pet transport crate we would use for housebreaking, Charlie nosed around, occasionally heading back to the kitchen to check his dishes and take a sip of water. We placed his new toys in the middle of the living room floor. He sniffed at them cautiously in the course of his wanderings, but he didn't understand yet that they were his to play with. Nan found some old towels to line the crate, and we placed it in our bedroom next to my side of the bed.

It had been a long, emotion-filled day. Just twelve hours earlier, I had no thought of owning another dog, and now I was the proud owner of a nine-week-old golden retriever puppy. I thought about how completely this would change our lives as I brushed my teeth and got ready for bed. Nan and I never had children, but we were suddenly the caretakers for a dependent young life. I hoped we would be able to live up to the responsibility.

Charlie had found a quiet corner in the living room for a snooze, and he barely roused as I scooped him up and carried him to his crate. I knelt down and placed him inside on the old towels. He was coming awake as I closed and latched the door. He put his nose up to it and pushed. The door just rattled. He put a paw up on it and pushed. Same thing. He realized he was locked in and let out a shrill whine of protest. I used a soft voice to try to calm him down as I crawled into bed. The whining continued, interrupted only by fits of pushing on the door and digging at the floor. I pulled the crate over closer to the bed so I could reach it lying down and put my fingers through the screen to let Charlie sniff and lick them for reassurance. Together we drifted off to sleep.

The next morning was a Monday, a workday. We hadn't been thinking even this far ahead when we decided to get a puppy. There was no way we could leave Charlie alone all day at home, so I put him in the crate, put the crate and some supplies in the back of the SUV and drove to my job at an Aspen-based software company. There were some surprised looks from my coworkers when I walked in carrying the crate with Charlie inside. Everybody wanted to see him, of course, but there was also some concern that the managers would not be too happy to have a dog in the office. I had put in my two-week notice a week before, after receiving an offer for a better-paying job, so I responded, "What are they going to do, fire me?" Not much was said by my supervisor, but it was obvious he was only putting up with the situation because he knew that it was only for a week.

That workweek went quickly. Like most puppies, Charlie divided his time between sleeping, eating, playing and going to the bathroom. Mostly, he stayed close to his crate, napping and chewing on his toys. He had quickly learned not to go to the bathroom inside his crate, but when he was outside of it, anything could happen. I needed to keep an eye on him for signs that he needed to go, like sniffing or going into that hopping spin, and then scoop him up and run him down the stairs and outside before it was too late. There were inevitable accidents, like the time he peed on the carpet outside one of the owner's office doors—a farewell present? And an incident when he was climbing up the stairs and was frightened by a coworker running up behind him. He loosed his bladder and scent glands while letting out an awful shriek. I had never heard of anything like that happening before, but Charlie seemed to calm down quickly as I held him, and there were no lasting effects other than his wariness of that particular coworker from then on.

When the workweek ended, that job was over. Charlie and I spent the weekend gardening, or rather I gardened and Charlie explored our yard and stuck his nose into everything I was doing. All the sniffing had a purpose, I discovered, as he tried to eat anything he found that smelled remotely edible: potting soil, gravel, sticks, grass, leaves and weeds. I also discovered that whatever he ate that was not edible passed through his system unaffected. To reduce some of this by-product impact on our lawn, Nan and I started to walk Charlie in our rural neighborhood, with the idea that he would use the grassy ditches that lined the roads for his business. Since there were no sidewalks, we needed to walk him on a leash for safety, but he wanted none of that. The first few walks were more like "drags," as Charlie dug in his heels and refused to cooperate. The willful nature Annie had warned us about was never more evident. In exasperation, I would carry him under my arm until he squirmed so much I had to put him down and drag him a little farther. We would eventually reach the intersection at the top of our hill, beyond which lay a dead-end road with no traffic, where it was safe to let him off the leash. Acting like he had just been released from captivity, Charlie would bound up the road, tongue flying and ears flopping. That image would make me smile until I remembered that I was going to have to drag him back home again on the leash.

There were no free days between jobs to spend with Charlie, working on the housebreaking, leash walking and basic tricks that were becoming a part of our daily routine. On Monday, I flew out to Stamford, Connecticut, for a week of training with my new employer, a financial software company. Nan was left at home to deal with Charlie on her own. I called her every evening to see how she was coping. She said that Charlie was being a good boy for the most part, with no accidents except for one. They were in the kitchen together, and she dropped a dish towel on the floor. Before she could bend over to pick it up, he sniffed it for a second and then started peeing on it. She said that she couldn't believe it. "What was he thinking?" I hoped it was just a marking thing and not a comment on her housekeeping.

The best thing about the new job was that it allowed me to work from home. Charlie and I would get to be together all day, every day. This was wonderful for our relationship, contributing to the strong bond we maintained throughout his life, but not so good for the concentration I needed to do my job effectively. Between naps, Charlie was a whirling dervish and I was the focus of his attention. To keep him busy, I would invent simple games that would take some time to figure out but that didn't require too much active participation on my part. Most of the games were variations on "fetch." Charlie was a retriever after all, and I wanted him to be a good one, unlike Rollie, who never showed much interest in the game. I would sometimes say of Rollie, "He's not a golden retriever; he's just a golden."

    At first, I would introduce an old tennis ball and tease Charlie with it a little so he would try to grab it in his mouth, but I wouldn't let it go. I would then roll the ball a few feet away from him. He would run after it, tackle it and grab it in his mouth. I would say his name and encourage him to come back to me. If he did, I would praise him, take the ball from his mouth and roll it a little farther away. Before long, he was bringing the ball back consistently, and it was time to make the game more complicated. I started rolling the ball out of sight. At first, Charlie would follow the path of the ball with his eyes, but when it disappeared, he would look back at me, as if to say, "Where did it go?" To his amazement, I would get up, make the ball reappear and give it to him. It didn't take long before he understood that "out of sight" did not mean "gone." I could roll the ball out of the room, under the furniture or down the stairs, and he would go find it. I could toss the ball into an open paper bag or put it under an overturned bucket, and using his keen sense of smell, he would figure out where it was. When it got to the point where we needed to bounce the ball off the walls to keep the game interesting, it was time to move it outside.

    Out in the yard, Charlie would take off running as soon as I started making a motion to throw the ball. He would snag it out of the air after the first or second bounce, using his "eye-to-mouth" coordination, and run it back to me. As he grew bigger and stronger, we increased the distance. I would throw the ball as far as I could, way out into the scrub oak woods that surrounded our yard and well out of sight. It would sometimes take several minutes, but Charlie almost always returned with the ball.

The best game we ever devised was what I called "moving fetch," or sometimes "Favre to Freeman," after the Green Bay Packers' Brett Favre and Antonio Freeman. Charlie and I would take a tennis ball with us on our walks, and I would throw it for him as we walked. Out on the asphalt road, the ball bounced predictably, and if I made an accurate throw just past his shoulder, Charlie would routinely catch it on the first bounce and return it to me. He quickly developed the reflexes of a shortstop, sometimes leaping high for the ball and other times short-hopping it but rarely letting it get away from him. If he took off running before I released the ball, because I was waiting for a car to pass or shaking off some of the spit, he would turn to face me and drop into a ready position. That reflex must be bred into retrievers, because I have seen hunting dogs do the same thing, but I certainly didn't teach Charlie to do it.

I did teach Charlie a number of other tricks though, from the basics like sit, down, stay and shake to operating a treat dispenser shaped like a gumball machine with a dog-bone-shaped release lever. Our friend Erik had lent it to us after giving up on teaching his own dogs to use it. When he was at our house to watch a Green Bay Packers game and saw how easily Charlie could operate it, he laughed and told us to keep it.

All the time spent together and all the games and training created a close relationship between Charlie and me. We were companions. We understood each other. I would talk to him like he was a person and he would respond like one, maybe not with spoken words but with the kind of nonverbal communication that is shared between two individuals who know each other extremely well.

Life with Charlie gradually settled into an easy routine. He was a member of our small family, and we treated him with the same love and respect that other families give to their children. Time passed, and like those other families, we were surprised to notice that our baby was all grown up. More time passed, and we were surprised to notice the gray creeping into Charlie's muzzle. He was getting older. The terrible unfairness of the difference in our life spans was impossible to ignore. Or could it simply be that dogs pack as much living into their short lives as we do into our considerably longer ones?

He is your friend, your partner, your defender, your dog. You are his life, his love, his leader. He will be yours, faithful and true, to the last beat of his heart. You owe it to him to be worthy of such devotion.

— Unknown

New Year's Eve

IT WAS NEW YEAR'S EVE, THE last day of 2007. I was teaching skiing that afternoon at Powderhorn, about an hour outside of Grand Junction, as I did most weekends and holidays during the winter. When my student and I reached the bottom of Bill's Run, one of the ski school supervisors, Lee, was waiting for me. "Your wife called. There's some kind of emergency," he said. "You can use the phone in Do's office." I turned to look at my student. Lee offered, "I'll take over your lesson. Don't worry about it." I apologized to my student and took off down the hill for the base lodge.

The rest of the run was a blur, my mind racing about what could have happened. A few weeks before, I had received a similar call. Nan was in the Emergency Department with terrible vertigo. The condition passed, and she had been fine since then, but what if she had suffered a recurrence? And what if she had been driving when it happened?

These thoughts hurried me along as I kicked off my skis and raced up the steps to Do's office. Do knew about the emergency and directed me to her phone. Nan answered her cell phone on the first ring. Thank goodness, I thought, maybe she's all right. She knew that it would be me calling. "John? I'm at the emergency pet clinic. Charlie has a tumor!"

"What? What's going on?"

"There's a tumor in his mouth. We were at home, and his mouth started bleeding. I couldn't get it to stop, so I took him to the emergency pet clinic on North Avenue."

"Whoa! Back up. What happened?"

"Charlie needed to be groomed and HBJ's Grooming was closed for the holiday, so I took him out to PetSmart. For a little extra, they offered to brush his teeth. His breath has been so bad lately that I said sure, go ahead. He was fine when I picked him up. But when we got home, I was in the kitchen and he was standing there looking at me, and blood started dripping out of his mouth. I wiped it up and called PetSmart. I talked to the groomer who worked on Charlie, and she said that she hadn't noticed any blood. She even went and checked the toothbrush she had used. The bleeding wouldn't stop so I got him into the car and drove him to the clinic."

"Where are you now?"

"We're in the parking lot outside the clinic. Dr. Becker looked at him. She was able to get the blood to stop by using some gel packs. Then when she examined his mouth, she found the tumor. It's about the size of a small grape. It's between his gum and cheek on the upper left side of his mouth. She said that the brushing must have aggravated it and caused it to bleed."

"Did she remove it?"

"No, she wanted to have it biopsied first to see if it's cancerous."

"Cancer?"

"She said it could be, but we won't know for sure until there's a diagnosis."

"Is she going to do the tests, or do we need to call Dr. Turrou?"

"She said to start with Dr. Turrou. We can call him on Wednesday, after New Year's."

"What do you think I should do now, head out?"

"Yes. Charlie and I will wait for you here at the clinic."

I hung up the phone and looked at Do. She said, "It sounds like you better get going." I thanked her and rushed out the door.

The drive back to Grand Junction was a distracted one. I thought about how much I loved Charlie and about how sorry I was that he was having this health problem. I thought about what I knew about tumors, which wasn't much: "malignant" was bad and meant cancer, whereas "benign" was good, or at least as good as could be hoped for given the existence of the tumor in the first place, and meant not cancer but rather some other growth. I thought about best-case, worst-case scenarios. The best case was that Charlie could have surgery to remove the tumor, and that would be the end of it. Good as new. The worst case was that Charlie had an aggressive form of cancer, that it had probably already spread to other parts of his body, and that he would be dead within a few months. That thought brought tears to my eyes. I am not a religious person but I whispered a little plea to the powers that be: "Please, let Charlie be all right. That's all I ask." I resolved in my mind to be positive, to take the most optimistic approach I could, as we faced the uncertain future.

When I pulled up to the emergency pet clinic, Nan and Charlie were standing next to her car in the parking lot. I parked and walked over to them. Charlie looked sheepish, like he was embarrassed by all the attention. Nan looked like she had been crying. I hugged and kissed her, then knelt down to look at Charlie's mouth. Nan directed me to pull back his left upper lip, and there it was, just above his back molar, attached to his gum like a small polyp.

"They didn't want to just snip if off?" I asked.

"No. Dr. Becker said there's probably more to it than what you can see there, so it's better to get a complete picture before doing any surgery. Do you want to go inside and talk to her?"

I stood up, keeping a reassuring hand on Charlie's shoulder. "I don't think so. I mean, what is she going to tell me that I don't already know just by looking at it?"

"Not much, I guess. We'll just have to get going with the tests on Wednesday and take it from there."

"What do you think we should do now?"

Nan knew what I was thinking. We had purchased tickets several weeks before for a New Year's Eve party at Bistro Italiano, our favorite restaurant. The plan had been that before the party, Nan and Charlie would drive out to Powderhorn in the late afternoon to watch the fireworks and the torchlight parade that were an annual tradition. My fellow ski and snowboard instructors and I would ride the chairlift to the top at dusk, then follow one another down a smooth, wide-open run while holding lighted flares in our hands, ending with a jump through the "ring of fire," a giant flaming hoop with the new year, 2008, burning at its top. The effect of nearly thirty people with bright red flames shooting out of their hands, snaking their way down a highly reflective ski run, was spectacular, like an enormous fiery dragon flying through the night. Dozens of people would gather on the deck in front of the base lodge to watch and cheer, and Nan was going to join them with Charlie.

Now that wasn't going to happen, and I was wondering if we should just forget about the party as well.

"Let's think about it on the way home and make a decision when we get there," she said.

When we arrived home, we rationalized that Charlie's mouth was stable and the tickets were expensive, so we decided to go to the party. We were among the first arrivals at 8:00, knowing we would never make it to midnight. More than anything, we just needed to step away from the situation with Charlie for a short time, and dinner out was that opportunity. We ordered champagne and toasted Charlie's health instead of the New Year. We watched those around us laughing and having a good time, but we couldn't escape the dread we were feeling. We talked little as we ate the wonderful food prepared for the occasion. We drank coffee afterward and then went home. It was about 10:30.

Charlie was waiting for us at the door, just as he always did. The same happy dog hoping for a treat for being the good boy he always was. We gave him some leftovers from our doggie bag, watching to make sure his eating did not cause the tumor to start bleeding again. We got ready to go to sleep, and Charlie settled into his bed under the window on my side of the bed. He let out the same contented sigh he always did when he lay down. In moments, he was asleep. I sat on the edge of the bed watching him, thinking how ordinary it all was and yet how suddenly different it had all become.

A dog is the only thing on earth that loves you more than he loves himself.

— Josh Billings

Tests and More Tests

When we woke up on New Year's Day, the events of the previous day seemed like a bad dream. The reality of Charlie's situation sank in gradually as we lay in bed, talking about what to do. Nan said that she would leave a voicemail with Dr. Turrou to make sure we got in to see him first thing the next morning. From there, we would do whatever he recommended. He was Charlie's regular veterinarian, and we trusted his judgment.

It was a crisp, sunny January morning, but there was no snow on the ground, so we decided to take a New Year's hike. After coffee, we drove over to the Tabeguache area, about a mile from our house in the Redlands area of Grand Junction, where we had moved in May 2005. Tabeguache is a great place to hike or mountain bike, a looping network of single-track trails over rocky sandstone terrain punctuated by huge boulders and gnarled junipers. Charlie and I had made it our mission the summer before to hike every one of the trails, and even though some were as long as ten miles and mostly up and down, we had enjoyed the accomplishment together. When the weather turned cold in the late fall, we stopped going to Tabeguache and stuck mostly to the asphalt bike paths in our neighborhood.

Now it was a treat to be hiking the trails again, and there was an obvious extra spring in Charlie's step. He was on the lookout for rabbits and chased several that had come out in the open to sun themselves. It was difficult to see how happy and carefree he seemed and then to think of the tumor growing inside his mouth. Nan and I didn't talk much. We just watched Charlie frolic and thought our private thoughts.

Dr. Turrou's assistant called back early the next morning after Nan had already left for work. She said that I could bring Charlie in right away, so I loaded him into the SUV and drove down to the Redlands Clinic. Dr. Turrou met us in the waiting room and knelt down to look at Charlie's mouth. He seemed surprised by the presence of the tumor, since he had given Charlie a complete physical and a clean bill of health just two months before. He explained the initial tests and then led Charlie away for a needle biopsy and chest X-rays. The results of the lab tests wouldn't be available for a few days, but he would have the chest X-rays developed by the end of the day when I came back to pick Charlie up.

Before I left, Dr. Turrou gave me a bottle of Graviola, a natural supplement that has been shown to kill cancer cells, and an article explaining its benefits in treating the disease. He said that it couldn't hurt if given in the proper dosage and might actually help if the cancer had already metastasized.

When I returned with Nan late that afternoon, Dr. Turrou showed us the chest X-rays. They were clear, indicating that if Charlie had cancer, it had not yet metastasized to his lungs. Then he had us look through a microscope at a sample from the biopsy. It was difficult to tell what we were looking at, but he explained that there are four common types of dog cancers, and to him, based on the dark particles that were visible in the sample, this looked like melanoma.

Malignant melanoma in the oral cavity is one of the most difficult cancers to treat because the tumors frequently recur after being surgically removed and because the disease spreads quickly to other tissues. A more favorable diagnosis would be either fibrosarcoma or squamous cell carcinoma. Neither cancer commonly metastasizes, so they are more easily treated by surgically removing the tumor and its surrounding margins. The worst possible diagnosis would be osteosarcoma, which attacks the bones, spreads quickly and causes great pain.

When the biopsy results came back the following week, Dr. Turrou called to tell us that they were somewhat inconclusive. The tumor was definitely cancerous, but it was unclear what type it was. He advised that we get a CT scan to show the extent of the tumor's growth beyond what we could see inside Charlie's mouth, and he recommended that we call the Orchard Mesa Veterinary Hospital to get one scheduled.

On Wednesday morning, January 10, I took Charlie in for his CT scan. To get accurate results, he couldn't be allowed to move during the scan, so he would need to be given a general anesthetic. I filled out the necessary paperwork and signed the anesthesia release, and then handed Charlie off to one of the veterinary technicians. She said that they would call me when he was ready to be picked up.

When I returned that afternoon, Dr. Clark brought Charlie out to the waiting room on a leash. He was a little groggy but very happy to see me. Dr. Clark then led us back to an exam room to look at a computer screen. Image slices of Charlie's head played in a sequence. At first I couldn't figure out exactly what I was seeing, but Dr. Clark pointed out how to distinguish bone and teeth from tissue and muscle, and then he pointed to the tumor. There was more to it than the grape-sized nodule clinging to Charlie's gum line. The tumor extended in an almost equal size up into the sinus area above the upper jaw and looked like a tiny balloon squeezed to fill a limited space. Dr. Clark pointed out that, like a balloon, the margins of the tumor were smooth instead of ragged, which was a promising indication that surgery could effectively excise the tumor without the need to remove too much surrounding tissue. He also pointed out the nearness of the tumor to Charlie's eye socket. If it continued to grow, it would put pressure on his eyeball and impact his vision.

Dr. Hugenberg came over and introduced herself. She confirmed what Dr. Clark had said and talked with me about Charlie's options. She said that their facility had the capability to conduct the surgery but that I should check back with Dr. Turrou to get his recommendations. Dr. Clark burned a CD of the CT scan and gave it to me to give to him.

Charlie and I returned to Dr. Turrou's office that same afternoon. He put the CD into a computer and examined the images closely. His conclusion was that even though we still did not know the nature of the cancer, it was going to be necessary to remove the tumor surgically, and he was not confident in his ability to do so. He recommended that we contact Dr. Marquis, a highly qualified veterinary surgeon at Tiara Rado Animal Hospital, and he called to set up an appointment for the next morning.

Dr. Marquis took an immediate liking to Charlie, scratching him behind the ears and commenting on what a handsome dog he was. Charlie groaned his pleasure in return and leaned into Dr. Marquis like he had known him forever. I had brought along the chest X-rays and the CT scan CD, so we took some time to look at them together. Dr. Marquis agreed with Dr. Turrou's conclusions but added his own opinions. He said that he could do the surgery but that the tumor's proximity to the eye socket was cause for concern. To get adequate margins around the tumor, it might be necessary to remove Charlie's left eye. I'm sure he could read the dismay on my face at that suggestion so he continued quickly, saying that before considering the surgery, we should really determine what type of cancer we were dealing with so we would know what our chances of success might be.

At this point, it was time for Dr. Marquis to ask the delicate questions: considering that Charlie was almost ten years old and a golden retriever's average life span is twelve years, what measures were we willing to take, and how much were we willing to spend? I looked at Charlie with watering eyes for some kind of guidance, and he gazed back at me with a look of absolute trust. "Whatever it takes," I said.

Dr. Marquis asked if we would be willing to take Charlie to the Animal Cancer Center at Colorado State University in Fort Collins. If he thought that they would be able to help, then yes, of course, I replied. He said that the only way to get an appointment was through a direct referral by a veterinarian, so he would call them on our behalf later in the day. He cautioned that it was a busy place and that it might be a couple of weeks before they could see us. Based on their evaluation, we would take the appropriate next steps when we returned from Fort Collins.

May I always be the kind of person my dog thinks I am.

— Unknown

Fort Collins Diagnosis

Dr. Marquis was right that the Animal Cancer Center would be busy. We were unable to schedule an appointment until Wednesday, January 23, almost two weeks from the date of his call. Fort Collins is about three hundred miles from Grand Junction, so we drove up the afternoon before and checked in to the Hilton just south of the Colorado State University campus. The hotel accepted dogs as guests and was located close to the Animal Cancer Center. It was apparent from the way they welcomed us that the hotel hosted many families in situations just like ours.

Our appointment was scheduled for 8:00 a.m. We arrived early, knowing there would be significant paperwork to fill out. After checking in and being given a clipboard full of forms and a stack of brochures, we looked around the large waiting room for a place to sit. There were already several groups of pet owners clustered at safe distances from one another to avoid conflict between their animals. Most of the animals looked subdued, not interested in meeting any other animals, and some were whining quietly. It was a sad place. We took seats near the check-in desk. Across from us was a woman with a large, three-legged dog. I concentrated on filling out the forms, while Nan read through the brochures and Charlie lay attentively at our feet.

After I turned in the forms and was told that a veterinary assistant would be out to see us shortly, I took my turn with the brochures. Some were objective about the treatment of cancer in dogs and some appealed to the emotions, cautioning that the needs of the dog should be weighed against the desire to keep the dog alive. As I read this, the idea that Charlie's cancer might kill him became a reality for me, and I started tearing up. I looked around the room at the other pet owners and saw that they were all at different stages in this same process. Some, like us, were hoping for a positive diagnosis; some were already past the first stage, like the woman with the three-legged dog, and hoping their dogs were now cured; and some were beyond hope, coping with the imminent loss of their beloved companions. Nan noticed that I was crying and handed me a tissue. She asked if I was going to be all right, and I couldn't respond.

A young woman in a scrub top approached us. She said that her name was Erin and that she was a veterinary student at the university. She would be our primary contact during the diagnostic process. After leading us down a hall to an examination room, she took a close look at Charlie and then sat down with us to explain what was going to happen. Dr. Dernell, the primary surgical oncologist, would perform a surgical biopsy on the tumor and then send a tissue sample to a laboratory that specialized in animal cancer diagnoses. It would take at least a day to get the results. Based on the lab report, we would evaluate our options, including surgery, which could be performed while we were there in Fort Collins.

Erin took Charlie's leash, and we stepped back into the hall. She said that she would call us on my cell phone later in the afternoon after the surgery was over and we could come back to pick Charlie up. The two of them turned left and walked away. Charlie looked uncertainly at us over his shoulder. I smiled and offered him encouragement, and then Nan and I turned right and walked back to the waiting room. Now there was nothing to do except go back to the hotel and wait for Erin's call.

We bided our time in our room, Nan reading the newspaper and me working on my laptop, though neither of us could concentrate very well. When Erin finally called, we both jumped at the sound of the phone ringing. Erin said that the surgery had gone well and that Charlie was awake and doing fine. If we could come back quickly, Dr. Dernell would meet with us briefly.

We sat in the waiting room for just a few minutes before Erin came down the hall leading Charlie. He whined in happiness when he spotted us and pulled Erin over to greet us. She handed me the leash, and we went to find an empty examination room. The one she left us in was more comfortable than the one from earlier. There were sofas, a kitchenette and a bookcase. Memorial plaques commemorating dogs who had died of cancer were displayed on the walls. Nan was petting Charlie and I was reading the plaques when Erin returned with Dr. Dernell. He was wearing a necktie with a white lab coat over it and gave the impression of compassionate professionalism. He invited us all to sit down and talk about Charlie's condition, while Charlie nosed around the room, no doubt smelling traces of other dogs who had been there before him. When he reached the bookcase, he discovered a basket of stuffed animals, intended for small children, and pulled one out to play with. Dr. Dernell and Erin laughed, and we explained that Charlie had his own basket of stuffed animals at home. Of course, none of those toys had any stuffing left in them, but then, every dog needs a hobby. Sure enough, Charlie was already trying to unstuff his new toy. Nan took it away, wiped the saliva off it and put it back in the basket. She gave him a Milk-Bone from a jar on the kitchenette counter to compensate.

    Dr. Dernell explained that he had removed the visible part of the tumor, and he brought Charlie over to show that just the stump remained inside his mouth. He said that there was a good chance the tumor would return and that the nonvisible part of it would continue to grow. The surgical procedure to remove the tumor would involve taking out at least four teeth and the upper mandible above them, plus the zygomatic arch that supports the eye socket and all of the surrounding tissue. He went to a cabinet and returned with a model of a dog's skull to better demonstrate what he was talking about. The visible effect of the surgery would be a flattening of Charlie's face, with his left eye pointing more outward than forward. I looked at Charlie and tried to imagine what he would look like after this surgery. It made me wince. Dr. Dernell said that our decision to put Charlie through the procedure would depend on the lab results. If the cancer was of a type that could be fully eradicated through surgery, then it would be worth pursuing. If it was melanoma or osteosarcoma instead, then all the surgery would do is slow its growth. Based on what he had seen so far, Dr. Dernell was guessing the cancer would be fibrosarcoma or squamous cell carcinoma, either of which could be cured surgically. The lab report would be available within twenty-four hours. He said that he would call us with the results and that he would support whatever decision we made.

The wait for the lab results lasted a full day. We puttered around the hotel room, took Charlie for long walks on the frozen fields behind the hotel and ate meals in our room. Late in the afternoon we called Erin to check in. She said that they expected the lab results before the end of the business day and that Dr. Dernell would call us personally.

At dinnertime the three of us drove down College Avenue to a Chinese take-out place we had passed on our way to and from the Animal Cancer Center. Nan went in to pick up the order we had phoned in, while I sat in the car with Charlie. As we were arranging the bags of food on the passenger-side floor for the drive back to the hotel, my cell phone rang.

It was Dr. Dernell. He said that he had received the lab results, looked them over carefully and regretted to tell us that Charlie's cancer was osteosarcoma. I turned to Nan and whispered, "Osteosarcoma." She gasped, threw up her hands and started crying softly. Dr. Dernell explained that there might still be some hope for a surgical cure but that he wouldn't know for sure without actually doing the surgery and evaluating the results. He said that he would discuss this and other options with us when he saw us the next morning. I thanked him and hung up.

Nan and I sat in the car sobbing. Charlie looked at us with a concerned but puzzled expression, not knowing that he had just received what amounted to a death sentence. We put our arms around him and each other and buried our faces in his fur.

"What are we going to do?" Nan asked some minutes later. "Can we really put Charlie through that surgery?"

"I don't think it would be fair to him," I said. "He wouldn't understand why we would be putting him through such pain and disfigurement. And if it didn't stop the cancer, then it would all be for nothing."

"I agree. Let's see what Dr. Dernell says tomorrow, but we'll need to tell him that we have decided not to proceed with the surgery."

When we were back in our hotel room, I called my parents, while Nan dished up the Chinese food, though neither of us had much appetite. I thought that I had gotten over the upset back in the car, but I choked up again with my mother and father. My mother was consoling, saying that Charlie had lived a good long life, that he knew that we loved him and that we should let nature take its course. My father, a retired radiologist with a long professional experience with cancer, asked me to describe Charlie's condition and Dr. Dernell's diagnosis. It was too bad, he said, but it didn't sound as if there was anything we could do that would gain Charlie much in the way of quality or length of life. We ended the call with both of them saying how sad they were for us but how happy they were to have known Charlie through the years, especially during the family get-together the summer before at my sister Jane's family's place in Seattle.

Nan and I spread Charlie's traveling blanket on the bed and encouraged him to jump up onto it. He hesitated because this was something he was not permitted to do at home, but we patted the blanket and commanded "Up!" until he finally jumped up and lay down. We sat on the edge of the bed all evening stroking him and telling him what a good boy he was, and then we got ready for bed and snuggled in on either side to be as close to him as possible as we all fell asleep.

We checked out of the hotel the next morning and drove to the Animal Cancer Center for the last time. Dr. Dernell and Erin met us and took us into another one of the examination rooms. We told them that we had talked it over and decided not to put Charlie through the surgery. They understood. Dr. Dernell said that the surgery could be expected to increase Charlie's life by only twelve to eighteen months. I asked how long Charlie might live without it, and he said, maybe three to six months, depending. He explained that the tumor would undoubtedly return but that we could begin a course of chemotherapy that should slow its growth and metastasis. This was something Dr. Marquis back in Grand Junction could help us with. There were also palliative measures, such as radiation therapy, that could be undertaken to reduce the pain associated with the bone degeneration of osteosarcoma, but there were no facilities in Grand Junction that provided the service. We would need to drive back to Fort Collins every few weeks. That wasn't practical, so we asked about pain medication. Dr. Dernell said that we should check with Dr. Marquis when we returned home and get a prescription through him.

We thanked Dr. Dernell and Erin for the care and kindness they had shown to Charlie and told them we would stay in touch to let them know how he was doing. They wished us well and told us to call if there was anything they could do. We drove off into the bright, sunny day feeling emotionally ill prepared to face the dark days ahead.

We give dogs time we can spare, space we can spare and love we can spare. And in return, dogs give us their all. It's the best deal man has ever made.

— M. Facklam

Living with Cancer

ON THE MONDAY AFTER WE RETURNED from Fort Collins, we called Tiara Rado Animal Hospital to make an appointment with Dr. Marquis to discuss Charlie's cancer treatment. When we met with him that Wednesday morning, he was not surprised that we had decided against the surgery. He agreed that it didn't gain us enough additional time with Charlie to warrant putting him through it. However, he thought that the chemotherapy could definitely gain us some time by slowing the tumor's growth and metastasis. We said that we had discussed it and that we wanted to begin a course of chemotherapy as soon as possible.

Dr. Marquis said that we could begin the chemotherapy right away, but we would need to leave Charlie with him for most of the day. First he wanted to take new chest X-rays to check for metastasis, and then he wanted to do an echocardiography of Charlie's heart to make sure it could tolerate the side effects of the chemotherapy. If those tests came back clear, then he would administer the first round of chemotherapy late in the afternoon. His plan was to alternate every three weeks between treatments of Adriamycin and treatments of

Carboplatin. The Carboplatin was known to have more serious side effects, so he would start first with the Adriamycin to see how Charlie reacted. He would call us through the day to let us know how things were proceeding. When we asked if there were any other side effects like hair loss, Dr. Marquis smiled and said that that side effect of chemotherapy affected only humans, not dogs.

It seemed that we had been leaving Charlie in the hands of other people frequently for several weeks now, but he was still not comfortable with it. As we moved to leave the examination room, he tried to follow us, but Dr. Marquis had him by the leash and he came up short, letting out a small whine when he realized he was staying. We told Charlie it was going to be all right although we both knew that we didn't really know how it was going to be, not today and not in the weeks and months to come.

Later that morning, Dr. Marquis called to tell us that the chest X-rays were clear. He had conducted the echocardiography, but he was waiting on a specialist at the local VA hospital to report on the results. Even if he didn't get that report before the end of the business day, he was confident about administering the first round of chemotherapy that afternoon.

Charlie seemed fine when we picked him up—a little tired but very happy to see us. Dr. Marquis said that he had been a good patient considering all the procedures they had put him through. The echocardiography report was still not in, but he expected it by the next morning and would contact us with the results.

When Dr. Marquis called, he said that the report showed that Charlie had a minor heart defect. His interventricular septum, the wall that separates the major halves of the heart, was unusually thin. One of the known side effects of chemotherapy was a thinning of the heart walls, so Dr. Marquis was a little concerned about this finding. He said that we could still proceed but that we would need to monitor Charlie carefully to make sure we were not overexerting him on our walks together. If he showed visible signs of tiring, like panting or slowing down, we would need to adjust the pace accordingly.

In addition to monitoring Charlie during our twice-daily walks, we stopped our games of moving fetch. We couldn't risk the trauma to the tumor that catching tennis balls in his mouth would cause. Of all the aggravations we put Charlie through, this one was the most difficult for him. He could not understand why there were suddenly no balls in his toy basket, or why when he found a ball during our walks that we would take it away from him instead of throwing it for him. It was heartbreaking to see how he reacted to losing his favorite activity. He would drop an ancient, dirt-encrusted ball at our feet and then dance and whine in anticipation of our throwing it for him. When we put the ball in a pocket instead, he would bark in frustration and jump up in an attempt to retrieve it from its hiding place. At first he thought that we were teasing him, but he eventually learned that we were serious and resigned himself to the situation. That resignation marked the beginning of the end for me.

Within two weeks of the first chemotherapy treatment and three weeks of the Fort Collins diagnosis, the tumor in Charlie's mouth had grown back. It was already larger than it had been when it was removed by Dr. Dernell. We called Dr. Marquis to request that he take a look at it, and he agreed to see us early the next morning, February 12.

Dr. Marquis was noticeably surprised at the size of the tumor and the way it was beginning to swell the left side of Charlie's face. We asked if there was anything we could do about it, and he suggested that we "de-bulk" it, that is, remove the visible part of it surgically. He said that we could have the procedure done right away if we were willing to leave Charlie there for another full day. Thinking the tumor would soon begin to interfere with Charlie's bite, which could cause him to nick it with his teeth and start it bleeding, we agreed to the procedure.

When we picked Charlie up late that afternoon, he looked like his old self again. The swelling was gone, and he seemed more energetic than he had been in several days. It could have been that he was happy to be going home after yet another day in an animal hospital, or it could have been relief from the pain he must have been feeling from the presence of the tumor in his mouth. Whatever the reason, it was good to see him feeling better despite the nagging thought of what could still be growing inside his head.

That nagging thought turned into genuine concern a few days later when we noticed that Charlie's left eye was watering. Nan would dab it with a tissue, but the watering persisted. I have experienced bad sinus headaches that caused my eyes to water, so I had little trouble imagining what Charlie must have been feeling. We would soon need to address the issue of pain management with Dr. Marquis.

The next week, on February 21, we were back at Tiara Rado for the second chemotherapy treatment, this time with the more aggressive Carboplatin. Before we left Charlie with Dr. Marquis for the day, we talked with him about Charlie's watering eye and the pain he must be going through. Dr. Marquis asked if there was any other evidence of pain, such as whining, lethargy or loss of appetite. We said no, that except for the watering eye, he was pretty much normal. Dr. Marquis commented on how tough Charlie was and how stoic he had been through all the poking and prodding he had been subjected to during his treatment. We appreciated his comments and nodded in agreement, but we were concerned that his toughness might be masking persistent pain that we should be doing something about. Dr. Marquis said that it would probably be appropriate then to begin administering pain medication. He prescribed Tramadol for the pain and a liquid sedative to help him sleep through the night. We started with both medications that evening after bringing Charlie home from his chemotherapy treatment.

The pain medication did not make an obvious difference in Charlie's mood or eating habits, but at about that same time, he started to lick his front legs obsessively. Nan and I devised different theories about why he was doing this: the movement of his tongue in his mouth helped to ease the pain, or he was trying to rid himself of the bad taste in his mouth. But it could have simply been a side effect of the pain medication. Whatever the reason, the licking brought the smell of the tumor out into the open, and it was foul, like the combination of an infected wound and rotting meat.

The terrible smell had us checking Charlie's mouth routinely for signs that the tumor was growing back, and it didn't take more than two weeks from the date of the de-bulking to see a new growth starting to form. More alarming was that the new tumor appeared to be growing even faster than before.

By the beginning of March, the tumor was about the size and shape of my thumb, and it filled the space between Charlie's teeth and cheek. The mass of it was gray and wrinkled, like a shelled walnut. The tumor occasionally oozed a reddish clear liquid that would drip from Charlie's mouth, especially after eating. And if he nicked the tumor with his teeth, it would bleed uncontrollably until it stopped on its own, since there was no way for us to bandage it or apply pressure.

Nan contacted Dr. Marquis to let him know how aggressively the tumor was growing and to express our concerns about the bleeding and oozing. He suggested that we bring Charlie in so he could inspect the tumor personally and also get another chest X-ray to see if the cancer was metastasizing. They scheduled an appointment for Tuesday, March 4.

When Dr. Marquis lifted Charlie's lip to look at the tumor, he groaned softly and shook his head. Nan asked if we should consider a second de-bulking. Dr. Marquis said that it was possible but that we couldn't continue the de-bulking indefinitely. It was addressing only the visible part of the tumor. If the part we couldn't see was growing as aggressively, then it was just a matter of time before we would need to consider giving up on treatment and letting Charlie go peacefully.

This was the first time that Dr. Marquis had mentioned ending Charlie's life, and it brought the reality I had first faced in the waiting room at the Animal Cancer Center that much closer. We were reaching the point of diminishing returns, where trying to control the disease and ease the pain start giving way to delaying the inevitable for as long as possible.

"How will we know when it's time?" we asked. Dr. Marquis replied that most pets give clear signs when they are ready to go. They stop eating. They lose interest in daily activities. They become withdrawn. Charlie was giving no indication of any of that. He was the same dog he had always been, except for the tumor. Dr. Marquis could see that this discussion was upsetting us, so he concluded that we could de-bulk the tumor a second time and take it from there.

Two days later, on March 6, Charlie went in for the surgery. This time, the removal of the tumor did not greatly reduce the swelling of his left cheek. His face had conformed to the presence of the tumor and it was going to stay that way, a constant reminder that it was just a matter of time, days and weeks now instead of months, before we would need to put Charlie to sleep.

The average dog is a nicer person than the average person.

— Andy Rooney

The Last Good Days

THE DAY AFTER THE SECOND DE-BULKING surgery, we drove to Moab, Utah, for the Canyonlands Half Marathon. Nan runs in the race every year, and she had submitted her registration and reserved a hotel room several months before Charlie was diagnosed with cancer. We go to Moab, which is only a hundred-mile drive away, at least a couple of times a year, so Charlie has been there many times. In fact, he traveled almost everywhere with us that did not involve flying, and he had become a seasoned road-tripper over the years. As long as he had his familiar bed at the end of the day, he was happy in any hotel room. We figured that this trip to Moab would be his last, so we decided to go despite our reservations about his condition.

After an uneventful drive, we checked in to the Gonzo Inn and settled into our room. We spread Charlie's travel blanket in the sitting area, even though we knew that he would probably be sleeping with us in the bed. At dinnertime, the three of us walked over to Zax Pizza for Nan's ritual carbo-loading. The restaurant features outdoor seating separated from the sidewalk by a low fence, and they don't seem to mind patrons tying their dogs' leashes to the outside of it.

As I waited outside with Charlie while Nan went inside to get a table, a family with a young girl and boy exited the restaurant. The kids stopped to pet Charlie, and the young boy asked, "What's wrong with his face?" Without thinking, I said, "He has cancer." The boy withdrew his hand from Charlie's head and looked up at me with an expression of disgust on his face. I immediately regretted being blunt, but I had been living with Charlie's illness for almost three months and no longer bothered to mask it with euphemisms. The boy noticed his family walking away and hurried to catch up with them.

Nan came back to tell me that she had a table for us outside, around the corner. I walked around the corner to meet Nan coming to the table from the other side of the fence. She petted Charlie while I tied off his leash and went inside. After we were seated, Charlie settled down on the sidewalk to watch the flow of people and vehicles, accepting an occasional pat on the head from passersby. When our dinners came, I snuck him bits of pepperoni and crust. Pizza had always been his favorite treat, the one thing he would beg for at the dinner table back home.

Nan was up early the next morning. She showered and dressed quickly and was out the door before 7:00 to catch a bus up to the race's starting point north of town on Highway 128, leaving Charlie and me still dozing in bed. It gets hot in Moab, even in March, so they start the race early to avoid the midday heat. Before she left, we agreed to meet later in the park where the race finished. I told her that Charlie and I would try to get some photos at the finish line. Before then, we were going to do our favorite Moab hike, the Hidden Valley trail.

Moab is bordered by two famous National Parks, Arches to the north and Canyonlands to the southwest, and like all National Parks, they don't allow dogs. Most of the trails outside the parks are overrun with four-wheel-drive vehicles, dirt bikes, ATVs and mountain bikes, so it can be something of a challenge to find good trails for hiking with your dog. Hidden Valley is perfect because it starts right out with a steep and winding climb up a virtual staircase of sandstone that makes it impassable for anyone but hikers, dogs and maybe horses.

When we arrived at the trailhead south of town off Arroyo Road, Charlie was whining in anticipation. There were only a few other cars in the parking lot, so we would have the trail almost all to ourselves. When I had my hiking shoes laced up and we were ready to go, I whistled Charlie over from where he was sniffing around and we headed up the trail. His energy seemed good, but I watched him closely as we worked our way up the grueling first section. Whenever he stopped, I stopped, and when he panted, I offered him cool water from my CamelBak. There were some stunted junipers at the top where the trail flattened out, so we took a break to catch our breath in their shade. As he rested, Charlie wore that wide-mouthed, tongue-hanging expression that is interpreted as a dog's smile. I smiled back at him and told him for the millionth time what a good dog he was. He narrowed his eyes in contentment for a few moments, and then it was time to see what lay farther up the trail.

We hiked the sandy track through the knee-high grass and sage that form a gray-green oasis between the towering sandstone cliffs on either side of Hidden Valley. There is a place where the valley narrows a bit and the trail winds through a short rocky section. I couldn't remember if the ancient Anasazi rock art I was on the lookout for was located here or at the next rocky section. I scanned the flat vertical surfaces of the giant boulders along the trail and decided that the petroglyphs were farther on. A short while later, the trail turned rocky again, and we mounted a small rise. Off to the right, etched into the dark patina of the pinkish sandstone were the prehistoric pictures. It occurred to me as I looked at the largest, an image of three ovals in a horizontal row, connected by lines, with a curved line coming off the top of the rightmost one, that I was looking at a crude map of the valley we were hiking through. The ovals represented the open grassy areas, the lines were the narrow rocky sections, and the curved line was the access trail from the main valley below. The moment felt timeless, as if Charlie and I could have been standing in that spot at any time in the last several thousand years. I need to get some photos of this, I thought, and posed Charlie in front of the petroglyphs. One of those images is number 14 in the photos section of this book, and one is on the cover.

As Nan and I felt our time left with Charlie getting shorter, we made a point of carrying a camera with us and taking as many photos as possible to preserve our memories of him. Of course, like doting parents, we had been taking frequent photos of Charlie throughout his life, but these would be the last, so they took on special importance and poignancy.

I would have liked to continue hiking up the valley, but a glance at my watch told me this would need to be our turnaround point if we wanted to meet Nan at the finish line of her race. Charlie was happy just to be out hiking with me, so he didn't mind when I gave him a long squirt of water from the CamelBak and then started back down the way we had come up. He stayed several yards ahead of me most of the way, following scents and bounding after rabbits. I was lost in melancholy, thinking this would be one of our last hikes together.

Nan was unhappy with her race finish because she didn't place in her age-group like she usually does, but the field was large and competitive so she didn't let it get her down.

We relaxed at the hotel through the afternoon and then snuck out for an early dinner, while Charlie dozed on his blanket. After a final bedtime walk, we moved his blanket to the bed and went to sleep, each of us tired from the day's activities.

Nan and I mail our family and friends a Christmas photo and letter every year. Usually the photo is a vacation snapshot, but I was determined that this year we would take a posed family photo, so I had finally bought a decent tripod. We took it and the camera with us early the next morning when we headed out Kane Creek Road to Moon Flower Canyon, a beautiful little break in the sandstone cliffs facing the Colorado River. There is a crack in the cliff wall there where the Anasazi placed a series of notched logs that allowed them to reach the top of the cliff, where it connects with the far end of the Hidden Valley trail we had hiked the day before. Like the cliff walls of Hidden Valley, there are numerous petroglyphs dotting the walls of Moon Flower Canyon.

We found a sunny spot at the base of the cliff, and I set up the camera and tripod. Nan held on to Charlie while I set the camera's timer and then ran over to sit next to them. When the shutter snapped, Nan and I were smiling for the camera, but Charlie was looking at some people who were checking out the petroglyphs. I realized that all the hundreds of photos we had of Charlie had always involved having a person behind the camera, usually saying his name to get him to look. Without that person, there was no reason for him to look at the camera. We could have asked somebody to take our picture, but we settled for what we could get instead, a nice-looking family photo but with a distracted-looking Charlie, which we decided not to use for our Christmas photo. The image is number 15 in the photos section of this book.

1. Rollie, our first golden retriever, at eight weeks in November 1991 at our home in Aspen, Colorado. Photograph by John Lichty.

2. Rollie in 1999 at the Maroon Bells, south of Aspen, Colorado, after crossing East Maroon Pass from Crested Butte. Photograph by Sue Witkin.

3. Charlie, at nine weeks, accompanies me to work during his first week with us in June 1998. Photograph by Heather Jurek.

4. Charlie in the front yard of our home in Aspen at about ten weeks. Photograph by John Lichty.

5. Charlie helping me plant the window boxes on our deck at about ten weeks. Photograph by Nan Lichty.

6. "39 forever," as the button says? Charlie, at eleven weeks, and me on the morning of my fortieth birthday, June 16, 1998. Photograph by Nan Lichty.

7. Charlie's first birthday, March 29, 1999. Note the hamburger "birthday cake." Photograph by Nan Lichty.

8. Charlie with the boys on top of Mount Massive, his first "fourteener," in the summer of 2000. Mount Massive is the second highest peak in Colorado at 14,421 feet.

9. Charlie with Nan at Aspen's Annual Fourth of July Parade, 2003. Photograph by John Lichty.

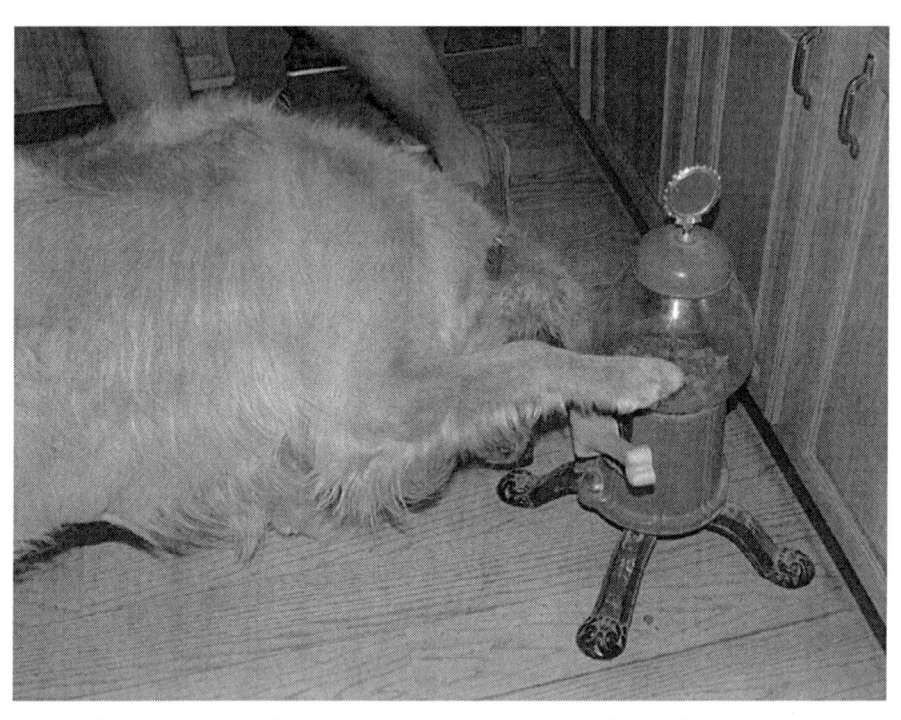

10. Charlie showing off how he operates his treat machine in September 2004. Photograph by Gene Hanson.

11. Charlie at the Lincoln Park Pool in Grand Junction, Colorado, in September 2005 for the annual "Dog Days" event. Photograph reprinted by permission from Gretel Daugherty and the *Grand Junction Daily Sentinel*.

12. Charlie relaxing at our home in Grand Junction in October 2006. Photograph by John Lichty.

13. Charlie at the fountain in the Seattle Sculpture Garden in August 2007. Photograph by Paul Snyder.

14. Charlie posing in front of the Hidden Valley petroglyphs near Moab, Utah, on March 8, 2008. Photograph by John Lichty.

15. Family portrait at Moon Flower Canyon near Moab, Utah, on March 9, 2008. Photograph by John Lichty.

16. Plaque created on the occasion of Charlie's tenth birthday, March 29, 2008. Note the missing nail on the left paw. Photograph by John Lichty.

17. Charlie at home in Grand Junction on his last day, April 6, 2008. Photograph by Nan Lichty.

18. Scout, at seven weeks, helps me celebrate my fiftieth birthday on June 16, 2008. Photograph by Nan Lichty.

19. Scout, at about nine weeks, taking a breather in his sling during a hike in the Tabeguache area near our home in Grand Junction. Photograph by Nan Lichty.

20. Scout, at thirteen weeks, at City Park in Iowa City, Iowa, during a road trip home to Wisconsin in July 2008. Photograph by John Lichty.

If there are no dogs in Heaven, then when I die I want to go where they went.

— Will Rogers

Denver Debacle

THE FEW DAYS WE SPENT IN Moab really were the last good days. The distraction of being away from home and its daily routines had put some emotional distance between us and Charlie's cancer. Returning home brought it back to our full attention.

Charlie was scheduled for his third chemotherapy treatment a few days later, on Thursday, March 13. Nan and I had spent many hours in recent days discussing Charlie's condition, and we concluded that the chemotherapy was having little effect. While it was true that the cancer had not metastasized, that fact seemed unimportant compared with the aggressive growth of the tumor, and the chemotherapy seemed to be doing nothing to slow it down. Less than a week had passed since the last de-bulking, but the visible part of the tumor in his mouth was already as large as a grape again. Nan called ahead to make sure Dr. Marquis would be available to talk with me when I dropped Charlie off for his treatment. She was scheduled to work that day and would not be going with us.

Dr. Marquis met Charlie and me in one of the examination rooms. He knelt down right away to take a look in Charlie's mouth, pulling back his lip to get a good look at the tumor and the area surrounding it. I commented that we were concerned about how rapidly the tumor had returned, when it had been de-bulked just seven days before, and that we didn't think the chemotherapy was working. Dr. Marquis stood up to speak with me. He replied that every situation is different. Some cancers respond to chemotherapy better than others. It was difficult after only two treatments to determine whether Charlie's cancer was responding or not. He recommended that we continue with the treatment for now and monitor Charlie closely. As the cancer took its toll on his health, he might suffer more severe side effects, in which case we should consider discontinuing the chemotherapy treatments.

"And then what?" I asked. Dr. Marquis let out his breath but didn't say anything. I knew what he was thinking. "How would it be handled?" I asked. He said that we could bring Charlie in or that he could come to our home if that would be easier.

I stared at the floor, trying to imagine the scene of Charlie's death. It was too much. I had tried to stay strong in front of Dr. Marquis during the two and a half months of Charlie's treatment, but now I found that I couldn't any longer. My eyes started watering and I couldn't speak. Dr. Marquis added that we weren't at that point just yet. We should see how Charlie responded to today's chemotherapy treatment and take it from there. I nodded, told Charlie to be a good boy and walked out.

When I got home, I walked into my office and sat down in front of the computer, but I couldn't think about my work. I turned to look at the calendar on the wall. I got up and flipped it to the next month, April. Charlie is going to die on one of these days, I thought. The end was no longer a future abstraction; it was real and it was approaching rapidly. That realization struck me like a punch in the stomach. I cried uncontrollably for several minutes, anticipating the grief that was soon to come.

As with the previous weekend, we had made plans for the coming weekend months before Charlie's diagnosis and thought it reasonable to try to stick to them. Peter Forsberg had returned to play hockey for the Colorado Avalanche during their attempt to make it to the Stanley Cup play-offs, and we had tickets for the Saturday afternoon game against the New Jersey Devils in Denver.

We left to drive down to Denver on Friday afternoon, the day after Charlie's chemotherapy treatment. He had seemed fine when I picked him up on Thursday afternoon, and he was doing well as we pulled out of Grand Junction. We had the back seats of the SUV folded down and Charlie's travel blanket spread out for him to lie on. Nan could reach him if he needed anything, and he did need occasional dabbing around his mouth. The tumor was oozing again.

Nan had given Charlie a pain pill and some liquid sedative before we left home, but they didn't seem to be easing his discomfort much. The noise and vibration of the drive were visibly irritating him, and he struggled to find a comfortable position. He must have bumped his cheek somehow because the oozing gave way to bleeding. Nan was alarmed by the sight of blood on the blanket and crawled into the back with a roll of paper towels to try to staunch the bleeding. There was no way to apply pressure. All she could do was hold a paper towel against his mouth.

With Charlie's head in her lap, Nan pulled out her cell phone and dialed the number of a veterinary hospital in the Denver area that she had looked up before we left. She explained our situation and said that we would drive straight there to have Charlie checked out.

It started snowing as we approached Vail on I-70. Farther on, Vail Pass was snow-packed, but drivers were slowing down, and there didn't seem to be any problems until we were a few miles outside of Frisco. Traffic in both eastbound lanes slowed and then came to a complete stop. Looking ahead, around a long curve, no vehicles were moving. A half hour went by but nothing changed. People started getting out of their cars and wandering around. Another half hour passed. Some cars in the right-hand lane eased onto the shoulder and parked. Their occupants got out and started walking up the highway toward the distant Frisco exit.

As we approached the two-hour mark, Nan started fretting about Charlie. She was still in the back with him, but the bleeding had stopped for the moment. She had given him another pain pill and some more liquid sedative after the phone call to the vet, and they seemed to be working better, but it could have just been that the car was not moving. Charlie seemed content to doze on his blanket, but she was concerned that he needed to pee.

Nan opened the back passenger-side door and crawled out. I needed to stay with the car in case we started moving again. She clipped a leash to Charlie's collar and encouraged him to jump down. He seemed uncertain and took several moments to think about it before he finally jumped down onto the snow-covered road. Nan led him past the shoulder, but when he left the pavement the snow was so deep that he sank up to his chest. As I watched from the car, Charlie took a few difficult steps and then fell over on his left side and started peeing into the air. Nan looked back at me and shouted for me to help her. I got out of the car and ran over to them, yelling, "What's wrong? Is he dying?" Charlie was moving his legs in a walking motion, perhaps believing that he was still upright. I bent down to get a closer look. His eyes were glazed. I said his name and he didn't respond, but he also didn't seem to be dying. More likely the combination of the medications and the drop in blood pressure from getting out of the car had caused him to pass out momentarily. His legs stopped moving and he turned his head to look up at us, but he didn't make any motion to stand up. I bent down, scooped my arms under his chest and rear end and stood up with him in my arms. He didn't struggle. I had been carrying him this way since he was a puppy, and he trusted me. Nan ran ahead to open the door as I carried Charlie back to the car. We got him situated on his blanket, and I checked his pulse by placing my hand on his chest. His heartbeat was almost undetectable. I placed my hand in front of his nose and could barely feel his shallow, rapid breathing. I thought again that he might be dying, but as we stroked his fur and talked softly to him, he responded by opening his eyes, lifting his head and panting lightly. Nan poured some water for him to drink. He still seemed a little dazed, but he appeared normal otherwise, considering his condition.

"We never should have done this," Nan said. "This whole weekend was a bad idea."

She was right, of course. The tickets were expensive and we didn't want to waste them, but we probably should have just stayed home. It was impossible to know that we would run into this terrible traffic jam, though. Or that Charlie would have a fainting episode.

"You know, there's no way both of us can go to the game tomorrow," Nan continued. "One of us is going to have to stay at the hotel with Charlie. And that's probably going to be me. Maybe you can try to sell the other ticket."

We had the radio tuned to a local station for updates. The announcer came on and said that a semitruck had jackknifed and tipped over just past the west Frisco exit, completely blocking both eastbound lanes. The state patrol and emergency crews had closed the road and were diverting traffic through town and then back onto I-70 at the east Frisco exit. This was hopeful news. We had been stuck now for almost three hours.

Way up ahead, cars that had been turned off were showing their taillights again and beginning to move slowly. We could have cheered. An hour later, we were on the other side of the accident and on our way again.

Charlie was dozing peacefully, but Nan was still concerned. She wanted to have him checked out by a veterinarian as soon as possible. She called the veterinary hospital she had spoken with earlier to tell them we had been delayed by an accident on I-70 but that we would be there within an hour. They were preparing to close for the night, so they gave her the address and phone number of the Wheat Ridge Animal Hospital, a twenty-four-hour clinic on the west side of Denver, near the Kipling Street exit. Nan called the clinic to get directions and to make sure they would be open. It was almost 10:00. The drive to Denver, which would normally take about five hours, had taken nine hours.

Charlie woke up when we arrived at the clinic, and we carefully escorted him inside. We told the receptionist that we didn't think it was an emergency but that we wanted to have our dog checked out by a veterinarian to make sure he was not in any danger. She led us into an examination room and left us with a clipboard of forms to fill out. A few minutes later she came back for the completed forms and told us the vet would be in to see us shortly.

The vet was a young woman, so young that we at first took her to be a veterinary technician. She looked Charlie over thoroughly, listening to his heart and lungs with her stethoscope and examining his eyes, ears and finally his mouth, where she took a good look at the tumor. We gave her the background on Charlie's condition and asked if there was anything we could do about the oozing and bleeding. She said that about all we could do was to protect the area and wipe away the blood and ooze. She gave us several packages of gauze squares to use as wipes and told us to call if we experienced any other emergencies while we were in Denver.

By the time we checked in to the Hotel Teatro in downtown Denver, it was 11:00. As soon as we set our suitcases down in our room, Nan started spreading towels over every inch of carpeted space. She didn't want to get in trouble if Charlie's oozing stained the carpet. I looked at the room service menu to see if we could still order something to eat. With all the commotion, we had not eaten any dinner. The kitchen was always open, so I called to order an expensive turkey sandwich we could share. Nan didn't have much appetite, though. When the sandwich arrived, she busied herself with feeding Charlie and making him comfortable on his blanket for the night. As we were getting ourselves ready for bed, she said, "Instead of trying to sell the other ticket, why don't you give Andy a call and see if he wants to go with you." Andy is an old friend from our Aspen days who now lives in Boulder with his wife, Angie. It was too late to call that night, but I told Nan I would try him in the morning.

We were up early the next morning with Charlie. He had been good through the night, leaving just a small stain on his blanket where his muzzle had rested. Nan took him for a quick walk down the hill behind the hotel to a small park where he could take care of business and then to a bagel place to get some breakfast for the room. When they returned, we made coffee and read the newspapers until it was late enough to give Andy a call. I caught him at home and explained our situation with Charlie and the terrible drive to Denver. He said that he had seen coverage of the accident on the ten o'clock news and that it must have been a mess. He was available for the game and could meet me at noon at the Pepsi Center. I said that it would be my treat.

Nan had not seen Andy for a few years, so she said that she would take Charlie and walk with me to the Pepsi Center. We took our time getting ready and then took a roundabout way through the Auraria Campus south of the hotel to give Charlie some exercise.

Andy had known Charlie since he was a puppy, and the three of us had once done an overnight backpacking trip to Snowmass Lake for a little fly-fishing. Charlie had howled when we tried to leave him at camp, so I let him join us as we fished the stream below the lake, but his wading scared away all the fish. Andy still managed to catch a few, but I didn't catch any. Charlie couldn't understand my frustration; he was having a great time splashing around and chasing sticks down the stream.

Andy was surprised when he saw the three of us waiting for him outside the Pepsi Center. He gave Nan a big hug, patted Charlie on the shoulder and commented on how old he was looking. The cancer was aging Charlie, there was no question of it, but Nan and I lived with him every waking moment so the change was much more gradual to us than it was to someone who had not seen him in more than a year. Andy understood that this would be the last time he would see Charlie, so he let him lean into his leg and scratched him behind the ears, saying what a good boy he was.

We said good-bye to Nan and Charlie and went inside to watch the game, but we spent the entire time catching up with each other. It was just as well because Peter Forsberg did not play and the Avalanche lost by a score of 4–2, coming close to being knocked out of play-off contention. As we departed, Andy wished me well with Charlie and I asked him to say hello to Angie. I walked alone back to the hotel, where Nan and Charlie had spent a quiet afternoon in the room after their own walk back. Charlie was snoozing contentedly after all the exercise, hardly stirring when I walked in.

We regrouped and walked down to the Wazee Supper Club to pick up a pizza and salad to take back to the room for an early dinner. Nan went inside to order, while Charlie and I stood waiting outside. In a scene reminiscent of the previous weekend in Moab, people came up to me to pet Charlie and then noticed the swelling in his cheek and asked what was wrong with him. When I explained that he had cancer, they were more sympathetic than the little boy had been. It could have been that he looked more ill than he had the previous weekend. He certainly seemed less energetic.

A good night of sleep after a fair amount of exercise improved Charlie's energy to the extent that he chased the squirrels around the

Auraria Campus the next morning when Nan took him for a walk before our drive home. I don't think any degree of sickness would have kept him from that sacred duty.

The more I deal with people, the more I love my dog.

— Oscar Wilde

Birthday

Nan and I had learned our lesson from the Denver weekend. There would be no more travel for Charlie. Rob, an old friend, was going to be in Aspen the following weekend with some friends for a spring skiing vacation, and he had invited Nan, Charlie and me to join them for the weekend, but that was clearly impossible now. I would have called with our regrets, but Nan said that I should go, without her and Charlie. She thought that it would be good for me to get away for a few days.

Rob was in his residency to become an emergency room physician. The ski vacation was a welcome relief for him from endless hours spent patching people back together, but he was nice enough to talk with me candidly about Charlie's cancer. Like my friend Andy, Rob had known Charlie since he was a puppy, and it saddened him to hear what he was going through. When I described the tumor, Rob grimaced and said, "Not good." He asked about the diagnostic procedures and chemotherapy treatments, and he nodded at my responses. "It sounds like you've done all that can be done," he said and gave a small shrug. I have seen other doctors do the same thing. It doesn't mean that they don't care; it's that they look at illness as a problem to be solved rather than as a misfortune to be suffered. The shrug simply meant that Charlie's problem could not be solved.

Nan was right. It was good for me to get away, but by the end of the first day of skiing, I was feeling guilty and missing her and Charlie. I decided that I would leave to drive home straight from Snowmass the next afternoon.

When I arrived home, Nan had something to show me. She knelt down next to Charlie and instead of pulling back his lip to show me the tumor, she pulled down his jaw and told me to look at the roof of his mouth. Next to the molars on the left side was a swelling like a blood blister, about the size of a nickel. "What do you think?" she asked, though we both knew what we were seeing. We had de-bulked the visible part of the tumor twice, and it had grown back aggressively each time. The part of the tumor we could not see, the part that had shown up on the CT scan looking like a small balloon squeezed into the sinus under Charlie's left eye, had been growing just as aggressively. Now it was pushing through the roof of his mouth.

"I think we're getting close to the end," I finally responded. I stroked Charlie's head and neck. He looked up at me as if wondering whether he had done something wrong. "Can you imagine how that must feel?" I asked. "I'll bet Charlie has the world's worst sinus headache. But you'd never know it. Just look at him." We both smiled at him. Looking relieved, he opened his mouth, stuck out his tongue and smiled back.

The first Christmas after Charlie entered our lives, almost ten years before, my sister Jane gave us an unusual gift. It was a paw print kit. The idea was to create a keepsake plaque by impressing your pet's paws in a tray of wet concrete. The kit contained everything needed, including decorative stones and a dog-bone cookie cutter. We had set it aside thinking we would do it one day. That was when Charlie was still a puppy and his days stretched out forever. Now we were running out of time.

Our move from Aspen to Grand Junction over Memorial Day weekend in 2005 was not a well-organized affair. Stuff was thrown randomly into boxes and loaded on a truck. We figured that we would sort it out in our new location. Three years later, some of those boxes were still not unpacked and were taking up space in the garage. We were pretty sure the paw print kit was in one of them.

When I arrived home after the ski weekend, Nan had another surprise to show me. She had found the kit. She said that she had had a hunch about which box it was in based on some of the other stuff that was piled in with it. She pulled that stuff out, and there it was on the bottom, still in its cellophane.

I read the details on the kit's box and figured it couldn't be too difficult. Charlie's tenth birthday was this coming Saturday, March 29. He and I would create a paw print masterpiece together to celebrate his big day.

After breakfast on Saturday, Nan went on a series of errands, and Charlie and I went to work. I poured the heavy bag of dry concrete mix into the square plastic tray and added the recommended amount of water. I stirred the water into the mix, but all it did was form clumps, so I added more water. The instructions said that the result should be the consistency of thick pudding, but endless stirring was only creating smaller clumps, so I added more water. As I stirred it in, the consistency went quickly to something like pancake batter—much thinner than pudding—and I thought, "Uh oh! Now I've ruined it!" The instructions said to "slake" the wet concrete, that is, to let it sit for a little while to firm up. That brought the consistency back to something that might actually hold a paw print but it was still too wet.

    I whistled for Charlie, and we stepped outside on the patio with the tray. I set it on the ground and pulled a patio chair over to sit on. Charlie was looking at me expectantly, so when I told him to sit and shake, I'm sure he was expecting a treat. Instead, I placed his right paw in the concrete. He reacted to its cold wetness by trying to pull his paw away, but I pressed it in firmly and then carefully lifted it out. I had a warm wet towel ready and gently wiped off his paw. Getting the left print was more difficult because Charlie would shake only with his right paw. I needed to lift his left paw from the ground, which almost caused him to lose his balance. I quickly made the print and then cleaned his paw. For being such a good boy, I stepped inside quickly to get him a Milk-Bone.

    When I returned and stood admiring our handiwork, I noticed the missing claw mark on the left paw print and remembered that Charlie had lost that nail a couple of years before. We had been playing moving fetch during our evening walk, and while chasing a tennis ball, he had stubbed that paw badly enough to make it bleed. When I checked the injury, I saw that he had torn off the nail. It never grew back.

    Lifting the tray carefully and placing it on the patio table, I tried not to slosh the prints away. There were bubbles rising in the concrete, and I tried to pop them and smooth their craters with a Popsicle stick without ruining the prints. Using the stick, I carefully pressed

Charlie's name into the concrete in large block letters. I didn't judge the spacing very well, and it came out a little pinched on the right side. To finish off the plaque, I used the cookie cutter to make a couple of dog-bone shapes and pressed in some of the decorative stones. You can see an image of the finished result in the photos section of this book. It is number 16.

When Nan returned, she was impressed with the plaque. "How did you ever get him to do that?" she asked. I think she thought that we did both prints at once, so I explained that we did them one at a time and that Charlie hadn't really enjoyed it, except for the treat when it was over.

The plaque now sits on our mantle next to the box containing Charlie's ashes. His old leather collar and tags are draped over the box, and on the other side is a framed photograph, a large version of number 13 from the photos section of this book.

That evening, I could smell that Nan was cooking something in the kitchen. When I went to check, she was frying a hamburger. Charlie didn't normally get "people food," but we had made a tradition of giving him a "birthday burger" every year. It was normally served on a small plate with a single birthday candle, and we always tried to get a photo of him with it. The trick was to get the photo quickly and blow out the candle before Charlie took his first bite so he wouldn't singe his whiskers. An image of Charlie's first birthday burger is in the photos section of this book. It is number 7.

The birthday burger this year would be his last, Nan and I knew. It made us both teary to serve it to him. We could barely make it through singing "Happy Birthday to You." Charlie didn't seem to notice. His focus was on the burger, his once-a-year delicacy, as Nan cut it into small, easy-to-chew pieces for him.

In one of the stars
I shall be living.
In one of them
I shall be laughing,
And so it will be
As if all the stars
Were laughing
When you look
At the sky at night.

— Antoine de Saint-Exupéry
The Little Prince

The End

On the Monday following his birthday, Charlie was scheduled to see Dr. Marquis again. This time, Nan would be taking him because I needed to go to Aspen for a meeting. The purpose of the appointment was to take another chest X-ray to check for metastasis, but Nan also wanted to show Dr. Marquis the newly discovered growth on the roof of Charlie's mouth.

When Dr. Marquis saw Charlie in the examination room, Nan said that he was surprised by how rapidly the tumor he had de-bulked just nineteen days earlier had grown back. It was bigger than thumb-size already. The sight of the new growth only added to the surprise. He commented that he had never seen such an aggressive cancer. And he said that considering what he was going through, Charlie's health seemed good otherwise. He was maintaining his weight, so his appetite must still be good. Nan said that she thought the cancer was affecting his ability to taste his food because he had been eating voraciously, as if he was trying desperately to find the taste. As they stood there looking at him, Dr. Marquis commented that Charlie didn't seem to be in any obvious pain; he wasn't agitated, panting or whining. "Charlie is one tough dog," he said.

The X-rays came back negative again. It was possible that the chemotherapy treatments were preventing the cancer from metastasizing, but they were doing nothing to slow the growth of the tumor. Over the next few days, it grew dramatically, more than doubling in size. By the weekend, it had swelled to the point that Charlie could no longer close his lips over it.

Sunday, April 6, began like any other Sunday. After waking up at about 7:00, I lay on my back in bed with my eyes closed thinking about the day. Charlie sensed that I was awake. He got up from his bed under the window and licked my elbow. I opened my eyes to greet him and stroked his head. Nan was already up. I could smell coffee brewing, so I got up and went downstairs to get a cup. Charlie followed me. The three of us sat in the dining area, two of us discussing what we were going to do that day. My plan was to get outside and do some yardwork. We were past the last frost, so I was going to get the irrigation system going as well. Nan needed some things, so she was going to make a shopping run and then clean up around the house.

Before we could do anything, we needed to take Charlie for his morning walk. Normally, one or the other of us took him, but on weekends, we sometimes both went. Out of consideration for Charlie, we had been shortening his walks and sticking to the neighborhood, mostly doing what we called "the playground loop," a route that takes us on an asphalt bike path out to a park located a short distance up our street, around the playground, basketball court and tennis courts in the park, and then back home. It takes just under a half hour, so it is probably about a mile and a half.

On the return leg, a man and a woman on mountain bikes passed us going the other way. The woman yelled, "Does he have a tennis ball in his mouth?"

Nan yelled back, "No, it's a tumor. He has cancer."

"Awww! That's too bad," the woman yelled as she disappeared around a curve.

Nan and I stopped to look at Charlie. The tumor was so big that it did look like he had a tennis ball in his mouth. When he smiled, his lip would partially uncover the tumor. It looked like a small gray brain nestled in the corner of his mouth, and it oozed continuously now. The smell, which had been bad for months, was now almost overwhelming.

After breakfast, I went outside with Charlie to see about that yardwork. The lawn was just starting to green up from winter, so I grabbed a rake to try to get some of the dead thatch out before it became too difficult. Charlie sat quietly in the grass watching as I worked my way around our small yard. Normally, he would have been dropping a spit-covered tennis ball at my feet for me to throw every few minutes, but those days were long over. While we were in the backyard, Nan came out with the camera and took a few photos, the last ones we have of Charlie. One of them is number 17 in the photos section of this book.

After the raking was finished, I sorted out the irrigation system, a series of hoses and sprinklers connected to the locally available irrigation water supply. It was after noon when everything was set up and tested. Charlie and I went inside for lunch and to watch the last Colorado Avalanche game of the regular season. They were playing the Minnesota Wild, the team they would face in the first round of the play-offs, so it was sure to be an exciting game.

Charlie was a good sport when it came to watching sports on TV. He didn't pay much attention to the games, preferring to stretch out close to me so I could scratch his ears and rub his tummy, but occasionally perking up for commercials featuring dogs and other animals. He didn't like it when I suddenly cheered or cursed; he thought that I was yelling at him, and I needed to reassure him each time that everything was fine.

The two of us were stretched out watching the game, me on the sofa and Charlie on the floor parallel to me, while Nan scurried around doing housework. She said that she was going to run the garbage out and opened the door to the garage. We heard the automatic garage door open, followed by the sounds of her talking with our neighbor, Jane. Charlie lifted his head to listen and then got up and walked outside through the open doors. He liked our neighbors, Dale and Jane, and always greeted them when he saw them out and about, but he didn't usually make this much effort. Jane told me later that as she and Nan talked in the driveway, Charlie sat next to her and leaned into her leg so she would scratch his head.

He came back a little while later and resumed his previous position next to the sofa, lying down with a contented sigh. When Nan came back inside, she sat on the floor with him and brushed his coat, something that he had been taking extra pleasure in lately. The hockey game was tied at the end of regulation and then again at the end of the overtime period. As the three of us watched, the Avalanche finally won it in a shoot-out by a score of 4–3.

I looked at my watch. It was already 4:00 and time for Charlie's afternoon walk. I grabbed a poop bag, clipped Charlie to his leash, and off we went for another lap around the playground loop, while Nan started on an early dinner. As Charlie and I approached the basketball court, there was a game in progress. It looked like some kids and adults from a large family picnic in the park were playing basketball, while others were watching from the adjacent hillside or playing games on the bike path. I didn't want to walk Charlie through the middle of them, so we turned around and started walking back the way we had come.

Charlie seemed agitated. After we had gone a few hundred yards, he stopped and put his head down. A string of pink drool dripped from the corner of his mouth. He rubbed his muzzle against his front legs like he was trying to wipe it away, and then he lifted his left paw to his face and made a motion like he was trying to push the tumor out of his mouth. He continued to brush the side of his muzzle until the tumor emerged from the corner of his mouth and ruptured. Blood poured out of his mouth. He became frantic, shaking his head, pushing on the tumor and rubbing his bloody muzzle on his legs. I stood watching, paralyzed by what I was seeing. "Oh, Charlie! Oh, Charlie!" was all I could utter. He stopped suddenly and looked up at me with an expression that said, "Why aren't you helping me?" I was at a complete loss. I glanced quickly around but there was no one in sight. I looked back at him. The look in his eyes made it clear he was finished. He had had enough.

"We have to get home, Charlie. Let's go home!" I started running and he ran with me, blood flying in all directions. This is it, I thought. This is the end. I burst into tears, sobbing so loudly that Charlie looked up to see what was wrong. The run home was endless.

When we reached home, Nan must have sensed that something was wrong because she was already coming down the steps. "What happened?" she yelled. I was crying so hard I couldn't talk. She said, "We need to get Charlie to the emergency pet clinic."

The SUV was parked in the driveway. We walked around to the driver's side and I opened the back door. Charlie's travel blanket was spread out in the back on the folded-down seats. I thought that I would need to help him but he jumped up on his own, circled and lay down, leaving a trail of blood on the blanket. Nan ran inside the house to call the clinic, and then crawled in back with Charlie to keep him calm. She told me to be careful as we made the solemn drive back to the place where our tragedy had begun just three months earlier.

As we pulled into the parking lot, there were veterinary technicians waiting with a stretcher. I parked and got out to speak with them. I didn't know what Nan had told them over the phone, but they were treating our situation like a life-or-death emergency. The bleeding had stopped on its own, so any emergency was over. I opened the back door to show them what was happening. Charlie stood up, walked to the edge, jumped down on his own and greeted the techs like he had been expecting them. His leash was still attached to his collar. I grabbed it and we all went inside.

The techs took Charlie away to examine him, while Nan and I stood at the receptionist's desk filling out paperwork. When the forms were complete, Nan suggested that we step outside for some air. Dr. Rumrill, the attending veterinarian, came out and introduced herself to us. She said that Charlie's condition was stable, and she asked for some background about the tumor. I told her a brief history, starting right at this clinic with the New Year's Eve discovery by Dr. Becker. I explained about the de-bulkings and the chemotherapy with Dr.

Marquis, and I related the afternoon's events that had brought us to this point. She listened carefully and could tell where I was leading. She asked if we thought it was time to put Charlie to sleep. I looked at Nan through teary eyes and saw that she was also teary. I replied that he had been through enough. He was ready to let go. Dr. Rumrill nodded sympathetically. She explained the process to us, told us there were forms we would need to sign, said she would meet us in an examination room, and then stepped back inside.

Nan and I leaned against the wall outside the entrance, alternately talking and crying. I told her that I felt like I was murdering my best friend. She tried to convince me that we had done everything we could, that Charlie had lived a long, full life and that it was time now. She hugged me and said, "He knows how much you love him."

When we went back inside, I told the receptionist that we would be putting our dog to sleep and cremating his remains, and she passed me a euthanasia form and a cremation form. I signed them and passed them back to her. She stood up and escorted us to an examination room. After a moment, Dr. Rumrill came in holding a baby blanket. She told us to get comfortable on the floor and that she would be back in a few minutes with Charlie. They were busy putting in an IV Heplock and washing off the blood.

Nan and I spread the blanket on the floor and sat down. I sat with my back against the examination table. Nan sat against the wall. Dr. Rumrill stuck her head through the door and asked if we were ready to see Charlie. We both nodded. She closed the door and then opened it again leading Charlie by his leash. He was overjoyed to see us. He ran over to me and tucked his head into my neck, moaning. Then he ran over to Nan and licked her face. Dr. Rumrill said that she would leave us alone together for as long as we needed and that we should knock on the door when we were ready.

We patted the blanket for Charlie to lie down but he wouldn't. He paced around the room, obviously nervous. It seemed like he knew what was happening and that he was working up his courage. I finally convinced him to lie down next to me with his back against my left leg and his head facing my feet. I buried my fingers in the ruff of his neck and stroked his chest, trying to calm him. He licked at the IV location on his left paw and panted softly. He turned his head and licked my bare leg. I looked up at Nan. She asked, "Ready?" I looked away and nodded. She reached out and knocked on the door.

Dr. Rumrill came in carrying a large syringe filled with a clear pink liquid. Charlie lifted his head like he was going to get up, but I kept my hand on his chest to hold him down. His heart was beating rapidly. She knelt down next to him, gave him some calming pets and took his left paw in her hand. She inserted the syringe's needle into the rubber IV cap and started pressing the plunger. Charlie reacted immediately, lifting his head to see what was happening. When he put his head back down, it clunked on the floor. The drugs were already acting. Dr. Rumrill pressed the plunger the rest of the way. Charlie's heart went into fibrillation for a few moments and then stopped. I felt his body relax under my hand. He was gone.

My best friend and constant companion was no more. The feeling of loss was overwhelming. Nan and I cried and stroked Charlie's lifeless body. Dr. Rumrill closed his eyes, told us we could take as much time as we needed and excused herself.

Nan and I sat with Charlie, not saying anything, for a long time. As I gazed at him, I thought back on all the wonderful times we had shared together. Was there ever a better dog? I didn't think so. I was so proud of him. Nan touched my hand and said that we should be going. I left my reverie and stood up, being careful not to disturb Charlie's body. I reached down to pet his head one last time. His fur was still warm. As we stepped out of the room, I looked back to see Charlie lying on his side on the baby blanket, looking as peaceful as if he were taking a short nap.

The world was conquered through the understanding of dogs.
The world exists through the understanding of dogs.

— Friedrich Nietzsche

The Lessons of a Perfect Dog

WHAT WAS LEARNED FROM OUR EXPERIENCE with Charlie, not just in the last three months but during the whole of his life? It would be difficult to answer that question simply. What is the influence of a living, long-lasting presence in anyone's life? In the case of a dog, especially a good dog, it is the equivalent of aspiring to an ideal.

In the introduction to this book, I referred to Charlie as a "perfect dog," but I didn't explain what I meant by that expression. To me, a perfect dog is a model companion. He goes with you almost everywhere he is allowed to, and he is calm and well behaved in all situations. He obeys your commands immediately and is respectful of your home and possessions. He does not bark except to alert you to a possible emergency. He walks comfortably on a leash and matches your pace. And most important, he is happy, healthy, loving and affectionate. In a word, the perfect dog is one you are proud of.

Charlie was all of this and more. His presence in Nan's and my life was for us, who have no children, almost like having a son. I even referred to him as "the boy in the dog suit." He couldn't speak to us, but we learned to read his expressions. In the same way, he learned to read our expressions and to understand much of what was said to him. He was a person to us and together we were a family.

Over the course of Charlie's life, I learned from interacting with him that even though dogs have fully adapted to living in the human environment, they have still retained much of their original "dogness," their viewpoint and their way of life. To truly know a dog, it is necessary to appreciate his perspective. In the introduction, I described this as a "meeting in the middle," where not only is the dog a reflection of his owner through the owner's training and influence, but the owner is also a reflection of the dog through his understanding of the dog's perspective.

Most of the original dogness qualities are ones we humans would be wise to emulate, for I believe the world would be a much better place if we all made the effort to learn what dogs could teach us.

Here are the lessons I learned from Charlie:

Be friendly.
Have you ever watched two good dogs who have never met approach each other? They do so with alert expressions and wagging tails. They give the stranger dog the benefit of the doubt. Of course, the next thing they do is the ritual sniffing, but after that they are buddies. The same goes for when a good dog meets a new person. They go up and lick the person's hand, expecting to be petted in return. In Charlie's case, his walks were regular meet-and-greets. He would make an effort to meet every dog and person we encountered, sometimes pulling me out of our way to greet someone. Most people would be flattered and laugh at his efforts. I would shrug and say, "He just loves people."

Charlie wasn't indiscriminately friendly with every dog and person he encountered. Sometimes he would be wary or even bark, as if to say, "Stay away!" The first few times this happened I didn't know what to think, but I learned over time that he was an excellent judge of character. The dogs he avoided proved to be unpredictable or aggressive, and the people he barked at acted strangely or had questionable motives.

Appreciate routine.
To humans, routines can be boring and repetitious, but to dogs, routines give order and meaning to their lives. Routines set expectations. Charlie knew how just about every day was going to play out: get up; go for a morning walk; eat breakfast; take a nap; interact with his humans; take a nap; go for an afternoon walk; eat dinner; interact with his humans; go to bed. Any deviation from the routine, such as a late feeding, was met first with puzzlement and then with whining. His world was out of balance. It needed to be set right again. Surprises were never good, especially ones that involved going somewhere in the car.

The most distressing sight to Charlie was the sudden appearance of an open suitcase on our bed. He would mope nearby, no doubt wondering whether it meant that he was going to stay with friends or that maybe he was going to go on a trip with us somewhere. Either option was upsetting to him because it would interrupt his daily routine.

Be patient.
Some people believe that dogs have no sense of time. I think it's more that they spend large amounts of their time either sleeping or waiting

for their owners to come home, so time is elastic to them. When we would leave Charlie home alone, we imagined him staring at the door, patiently waiting for us to return and thinking, "This, too, will pass." In reality, he was probably asleep within five minutes and didn't wake up until he heard the car in the driveway. Good things happen to dogs who wait, though. We normally brought him home a treat from wherever we went.

Communicate.
There is a greeting card that has on its front a dozen cartoon faces of a golden retriever. Under each one is a label for a different mood, like "angry," "depressed" and "bored." The caption reads, "The many moods of the golden retriever." The joke is that the cartoon faces are all identical. They all show a happy, smiling dog. Golden retrievers have a reputation for always being upbeat and enthusiastic, but that doesn't mean they are shallow and one-dimensional. They have expressive faces that communicate every thought and feeling. Charlie could speak paragraphs with just his eyebrows. And sometimes his look simply said, "Are you going to finish eating that?"

Pay attention.
Everyone knows that dogs have a keen sense of smell. In fact, as hunting animals, all of their senses are keen. Unlike humans, who are usually so preoccupied that they miss most of their sensory clues, dogs are always on alert, filtering sensory clues even when they are asleep. Charlie would wake up from the smell of Nan cooking and wander into the kitchen hoping some food had fallen on the floor.

When we were outside, I learned to take my cues from Charlie. If he suddenly looked in a certain direction or pricked up his ears, I would stop and look where he was looking. I was standing with Charlie and a friend at a campfire one night when Charlie started barking ferociously. The friend and I looked but didn't see or hear anything. A few seconds later, a man stepped into the light of the fire. He wasn't threatening, but we would have had plenty of warning if he had been.

Charlie kept track of who was at home and who was not. If he heard noise at the door and knew that one of us was out, he would run to the door to greet that person coming home. But if there was noise at the door and he knew we were both at home, he would run to the door and bark continuously until we proved to him that there was no threat. Delivery people were sometimes intimidated, but we appreciated what a good watchdog Charlie was.

Be loyal.
Dogs are social animals. In the wild, they live in packs. They know who their pack mates are and they are loyal to them. In the human environment, dogs form vicarious packs but the loyalties are the same. It takes serious mistreatment for a dog to willingly leave its home, and there are many stories of dogs finding their way home after long separations. We would sometimes leave Charlie with friends when we traveled and would wonder if he thought that the arrangement was permanent, but when we returned there was never any question that he was going home with us. We were his people.

Don't be too serious.
Throughout his life, Charlie retained the carefree attitude of his puppyhood. It was not an accident that his nicknames included "Goofball," "Nut Cake" and "Fruit Loop." He was a playful, fun-loving

dog to the very end. Several times a day, he would approach me with a well-worn tennis ball or a partially unstuffed stuffed animal inviting me to play. If I didn't take the time, he would go off and play by himself, inventing crazy games to keep himself entertained. We would sometimes find his toys in the most unusual places and scratch our heads wondering how he had put them there. And sometimes we would watch as he carefully put a toy back in his toy basket and selected a different one to play with.

Be brave.
Part of being brave is trusting in a positive outcome. For a dog, who does not think about outcomes, the trust is in you. When you pull into the animal hospital parking lot and your dog bravely walks into the waiting room despite terrible past experiences, he is being brave because he trusts you.

In the summer of 2006, when he was eight years old, Charlie was tackled by another dog while chasing a tennis ball and blew out his left knee. We wanted him to be as good as new again, so we put him through a surgical procedure called a tibial plateau leveling osteotomy. It was invasive and painful, and the recovery was long and slow, but we sensed that he knew we were trying to fix his knee, so he was a trouper throughout the process. Within a few months of the accident, we were playing moving fetch again as though it had never happened.

Appreciate nature.
Owning a dog is probably the number one reason why most people ever go for a walk. The side benefit is that those walks get you outside,

where you can appreciate nature firsthand. And being with a dog in nature is like experiencing it with fresh eyes.

In August 2007, Charlie and I took a road trip up to Seattle, where my sister Jane was hosting a family get-together at her family's vacation home on Whidbey Island. On one of the mornings when Charlie and I walked down to the water, the tide was out, so we walked across the seaweed and mussels to Baby Island, a tiny uninhabited island about three hundred yards offshore. As we walked up on the sandy beach, we heard some strange bleating sounds and looked over a dune to see two Harbor seal pups left on shore while their parents searched for food. Charlie kept his distance, alternately looking at the pups and then looking at me as if to ask, "What *are* those things?" I had to laugh about his sense of wonder at seeing these new creatures.

Be obedient.
For a dog, obedience is more than responding to voice commands and hand signals. In a close relationship, a dog will also respond to your emotions. A dog's perception of danger is different from a human's, so it is critical that he take his cues from you and react accordingly regardless of their source.

When we were living in Aspen, I came home from work one autumn afternoon and let Charlie out of the house to take care of business while I got ready to take him for a walk. Within a few seconds of closing the door behind him, Charlie started barking as if his life depended on it. I opened the door again and there was Charlie up on the hill behind the house, crouched and barking at a large black bear sitting on its haunches less than ten feet away from him. I groaned loudly at the sight of this potentially disastrous situation, and Charlie heard me, looked at me and sensed my alarm. He slowly backed away to a safe distance. I shouted, "Charlie, come!" and he came trotting back to me looking a little sheepish but otherwise proud of himself. We stood together and watched as the bear rolled forward onto its paws and slowly sauntered away up the hill.

Go for long walks.
One of the best things about a large-breed dog like a golden retriever is that they have no trouble keeping up with you on a long walk, a strenuous hike or even a mountain climb. And nothing helps build a strong relationship better than doing these activities together.

Charlie came into our lives near the end of my successful quest to climb all fifty-four of Colorado's fourteen-thousand-foot peaks, but I repeated a couple of the easier ones just to do them with him. We climbed Mount Massive together twice and shared the same sense of accomplishment each time while standing on the summit, though Charlie was probably thinking, "Now let's get going back down!" There is an image of the first climb in the photos section of this book. It is number 8.

Take naps.
In keeping with not being too serious, naps were an important part of Charlie's life. I used to envy his ability to sleep anywhere at any time. He could sleep a full night, go for a morning walk, eat breakfast and then go right back to sleep. Maybe it was an aid to digestion. To me, it was a sign of how relaxed he was, how untroubled he was compared with the concerns of the human condition. It was a sense of cool I could never achieve no matter how many naps I took.

The examples of Charlie's dogness qualities reinforce what a perfect dog he was. Like a successful older sibling, he was a hard act to follow. I tried hard to live up to the example he set and the expectations I felt he had for me, and I believe I am a better person because of it. People would ask what I did to deserve such a good dog. All I could think to say was that we spent most of our time together, so we had a strong relationship and we understood each other. It was that simple.

Most of what you need to know to be a good person and live a full life you can learn from your dog.

— John Lichty

Reflections

AT THE BEGINNING OF EVERY CHAPTER in this book is a quote about dogs. Some are familiar and some are obscure; some are by famous people and some are by unknowns. This chapter is devoted to quotes about one particular dog by the people who knew him.

> I always think of him as CHARLIE!!! because that was usually the way he needed to be addressed. CHARLIE!!! was a 24/7 example of the importance of fully embracing life, which he always did, whether on a long hike or just rushing to greet and smother anyone arriving at the Lichty home. CHARLIE!!! also had the best loving, caring parents possible, and his demeanor reflected that. He lived a full life, and we are all richer for it.
>
> — Andy, friend

During the family gathering in Seattle, Charlie was such a large presence that he was like a member of the family.

— Dad

I used to enjoy watching him hide behind cars and bushes while he waited for John to throw the ball. He would crouch down and get all "stealthy" pretending we couldn't see him.

— Dale, friend and neighbor

Charlie was the epitome of "man's best friend" to John and Nan. He will be missed.

— Dave B., friend

Charlie was the ultimate companion. Whether on an all-day hike, chasing a ball in the yard or waiting patiently in the car for John and Nan to return from a margarita (or two) at Eric's Bar in Aspen, he was just happy to be a core part of their lives.

— Dave K., friend

Charlie (Charles Edward Rutherford IV) was born to a well-to-do family in Rhode Island. Charles was always easygoing and gregarious. Early it was obvious that Charles was extremely intelligent, getting his nose in just about everything. He soon developed a knack for music. He longed for a career singing, but unfortunately his voice was too much of a bark. He also loved the piano, but unfortunately he was born with very short fingers and no thumbs. He would have loved to attend Juilliard, and did apply at various prestigious schools, but alas, each and every time he was turned away by someone singing in a very low voice, "No Dogs Allowed!"

Eventually, Charles settled in Aspen, Colorado, where he met up with John and Nan Lichty. They provided him a great home with lots of love, land for him to frolic and an endless supply of tennis balls. Finally, feeling that Charles was far too formal, they simply referred to him as Charlie.

I had the privilege of seeing Charlie's intelligence in action by seeing him hit a lever that would deliver dog treats. I think I've seen this same trick done in Las Vegas, but with much less consistent results.

— Gene, friend

Charlie was lovable from start to finish. For me he was a welcome clown who was always a good guest at our Aspen condo even when confronted with the bear in the parking lot.

— Hope, friend

Charlie was a really happy dog. And he was never happier than when he had a tennis ball and a place to swim.

— Jack, brother-in-law

I was touched that on his last day he made a special effort to say good-bye to me.

— Jane, friend and neighbor

Charlie was a real trouper—and he lived to play. He stayed with John at my place in Seattle one summer, in a tent that John pitched on my small patio, in deference to my elderly cats, Ursula and Charlotte, the two situated safely on the other side of the glass back door. (When they did meet face-to-face, Charlie showed no interest whatsoever.) My sister, Susan, and I had decided to find Charlie a patch of grass and grabbed his ball chucker and walked with him down to the park, to a big open field near some tennis courts. Little did we know how seriously he took this game. He ran at full speed after every ball we heaved, never relenting. Finally, after retrieving one poorly thrown ball, he trotted off in another direction. We thought that the game had ended. But no, he had spotted a clean new tennis ball that had been hit over the fence. He dropped the old slimy ball and picked up the bright green one, adhering to a kind of take-one-leave-one etiquette. And the game continued, until Susan and I were worn out.

— Jane, sister

Charlie was simply a big golden bundle of love. A beautiful, gentle and smart dog, he was seldom without his grungy weathered tennis ball clamped in his mouth just waiting for the opportunity to play. Gentle nudges and sniffs with his nose, a great pool diver, and a tail that seemed to never stop wagging… a buddy like Charlie only comes along once in a man's lifetime. He was a canine companion of the first magnitude. Charlie surely will be forever missed.

— Jim, friend and coworker

Charlie was one tough dog on our Mount Massive climb!

— Keith, friend

We were looking after Charlie while John and Nan were out of town, and there was an open house going on in our neighborhood in Aspen. The front door of the house was open and you could see a fountain in the entryway. Charlie ran inside and jumped right into it.

— Lori, friend

My fondest memory of Charlie was the time we spent at John and Nan's home on Medicine Bow Road in Aspen during a very snowy week. We were all out in the driveway, where John demonstrated the fine art of tossing a tennis ball. Charlie was very good at catching the ball in midair or retrieving the ball from a snow bank. When it was my turn, I tossed the ball and it probably went about ten feet. Charlie turned and gave me that "you've got to be kidding" look. We all had a good laugh.

— Mom

I first met him in John's sister Jane's backyard in Seattle. He was hiding behind the house with only his nose peering around the corner. It was as if he was saying, "Glad to meet you—Charlie is my name, playful is my game."

— Paul, friend

The thing I remember the most about Charlie was how he seemed to recognize his circle of people. Though he was friendly to everyone, he seemed to hold certain people in higher appreciation and greeted them accordingly. It was fun having him at the eBay consignment store, and I know my golden, Dakota, knew him as a friend.

— Phillip, friend

By the way they greeted each other in the neighborhood, I think Charlie and our golden retriever, Chelsea, both knew that the other was dying. Chelsea died just a couple of months after Charlie did.

— Rich, friend and neighbor

Charlie was magnanimous, a super dog; an archetype. When people wax sentimental about the joys of dog companionship, the dog they see in their mind's eye—whether they know it or not—is Charlie. He had all the qualities one seeks in a canine friend—playfulness and energy, loyalty, and an astounding willingness to cooperate. He also possessed the requisite physical characteristics necessary for doggy greatness—long, soft fur that was ideal for petting, floppy ears and a comically bushy tail; he was cute and approachable, yet he retained a strong element of regality. Charlie was independent, strong-willed, and mischievous; qualities which, in proper amounts, give dogs a wonderful personality, one that is at times, needfully onerous—in a solid relationship, all members must work. As a lover of dogs, it would be difficult for me to disparage anyone, but when I think of all the dogs that I've known, Charlie is certainly one of my favorites.

— Rob, friend

I remember Charlie's joy at seeing me for the first time after a long while with the sweet sound of a loving whimper as he would rub up against me. It always warmed my heart that he recognized me and knew who I was.

— Robin, friend

I had an aggressive dog in the shop one day when Charlie was there. When the dog made a move toward me, Charlie stepped between us to protect me.

— Shawn, owner of
HBJ's Grooming

He was such a great dog!

— Sue, sister-in-law

I loved Charlie's "puppy hugs" and I always tell people about them. Puppy Hug: legs together, slap your thighs and call Charlie's name, and he would come over and push his head into your legs, wag his tail and call out "a-wooo wooo wooo" while you scratched his back. It made my heart melt!

— Susan, sister

In the beginning, man lived together with the animals. But a crack developed in the earth, leaving man on one side and the animals on the other. At the last moment, before the crack became too wide, the dog jumped across.

— Creation Myth

Epilogue: Raising Scout

THIS BOOK DID NOT START OUT solely as a memoir. The first draft was written as an instructional guide about what it takes to have a perfect dog, using Charlie as the example. But then Nan gave me a golden retriever puppy for my fiftieth birthday, and I came to a humbling realization. Before I get to that, a little background is in order.

The immediate emptiness I felt over losing Charlie gave way a few days after his death to a deep and lasting depression. I couldn't concentrate; I couldn't sleep; I couldn't laugh. I just kept thinking about Charlie and wondering if he would still be alive if we had handled his treatment differently, or if we could have somehow prevented his illness in the first place. He had trusted me to help him, and I felt that I had let him down.

Almost two months after Charlie's death, I was in the Washington, D.C., area for a work-related conference and stayed with my friend Curt and his family in Falls Church, Virginia. While I was there, I intercepted an email message that was intended for Nan. It was from a golden retriever adoption group. When I called to check in, I asked her what she was up to. She admitted that she was trying to get me a new dog to help ease my sorrow over Charlie. I didn't know what to say. I told her to let me think about it before she did anything.

Was I ready for another dog? It seemed way too soon. It also seemed disrespectful to Charlie's memory. The grief over his loss was something I didn't think I could ever go through again. I had expected that I would never have another dog, but then Nan emailed me to say that the golden retriever adoption group did not currently have any dogs to adopt, so she was looking at puppies and had found a breeder in the Provo, Utah, area. She included a link to their website. As I had thought ten years before with Charlie and his littermates, it couldn't hurt to look. There were several images of the regal-looking sire, Titus. And there was an announcement of a new litter born to his dam, Annie, on April 28.

When Nan and I talked next, I told her I would give it some more thought and discuss it with her when I returned home. Instead of paying attention to the speakers at the conference, I found myself thinking about puppies and wondering what Charlie would think. I concluded that he would want me to be happy again, even if it meant bringing a new dog into my life.

Nan could tell what I had decided when she picked me up at the airport on Wednesday night, and it made her happy to see me happy. She called the breeder the next day to see about taking a look at Titus and Annie's puppies. Heather, the breeder, said that she could meet us on Saturday morning, so we drove up to Provo on Friday evening.

The puppies were not quite four weeks old, but they were old enough to be completely adorable and extremely rambunctious, falling all over one another and then falling asleep in piles. We were the first to look at them, so we would have the pick of the litter. I narrowed it down to one of two males and was leaning toward the lighter-colored one based on his outgoing personality, but Nan convinced me to go with the darker one simply because he was cuter. I took Rollie's puppy collar, which I had held on to for seventeen years, and put it around the puppy's neck. Nan gave Heather a deposit check to seal the deal, and we were on our way to owning our third golden retriever. Unlike Rollie and Charlie, this one would have a more traditional dog name: Scout. One of my favorite books is *To Kill a Mockingbird* by Harper Lee, so I like to think that Scout is named after the story's narrator.

Three weeks later, a few days before he would be seven weeks old, we went to pick up Scout. It was a long drive home for the little guy, but he slept through most of it. We stopped every hour to see if he needed to pee, and he did a few times. We figured that he would be hungry when we arrived home, so we fed him a little puppy chow mixed with warm water. He ate it quickly and then promptly threw it back up. A little while later, he pooped wetly on the carpet. Something wasn't right. I picked him up and held him, and he felt thin and fragile in my hands. I asked Nan if she knew anything about puppies failing to thrive, as sometimes happens with human newborns. She said that it was just anxiety over being separated from his mother and littermates. She was probably right, but it made me feel that even after two previous puppies, I didn't really know what I was doing.

Scout's condition improved quickly, but the nagging doubt persisted. We were able to housebreak him quickly, but the rest of the training went terribly. At the sight of a Milk-Bone, Scout would jump straight up and down, barking like crazy. He wouldn't pay attention to what I was trying to teach him; he just wanted that treat and he wanted it now. It took several days to get him to respond to his name and a couple of weeks to get him to sit. He liked to play with his toys, but he showed no interest in fetching. I didn't remember Charlie's training being anything close to this difficult.

As I mentioned, I was writing the first draft of this book during this period, the draft that would provide instructions on how to have the perfect dog. The more I sat at my computer staring at that manuscript, the more I realized that I was no dog expert. Scout was clear evidence of that. I abandoned my first draft and started over, with the idea that I would simply tell Charlie's story, the story of a dog who didn't need much more from me than my time and attention to become what he was, a perfect dog.